Osprey Modelling • 32

Modelling the Messerschmitt Bf 109B/C/D/E

Brett Green

Consultant editor Robert Oehler • *Series editors* Marcus Cowper and Nikolai Bogdanovic

First published in 2006 by Osprey Publishing
Midland House, West Way, Botley, Oxford OX2 0PH, UK
443 Park Avenue South, New York, NY 10016, USA
E-mail: info@ospreypublishing.com

ISBN-10: 1 84176 940 1
ISBN-13: 978 1 84176 940 0

Page layout by Servis Filmsetting Ltd, Manchester, UK
Typeset in Monotype Gill Sans and ITC Stone Serif
Index by Alison Worthington
Originated by United Graphics Pte Ltd, Singapore
Printed and bound in China by Bookbuilders

06 07 08 09 10   10 9 8 7 6 5 4 3 2 1

A CIP catalogue record for this book is available from the British Library.

FOR A CATALOGUE OF ALL BOOKS PUBLISHED BY OSPREY MILITARY
AND AVIATION PLEASE CONTACT:

NORTH AMERICA
Osprey Direct, c/o Random House Distribution Center, 400 Hahn Road, Westminster,
MD 21157, USA
E-mail: info@ospreydirect.com

ALL OTHER REGIONS
Osprey Direct UK, P.O. Box 140, Wellingborough, Northants, NN8 2FA, UK
E-mail: info@ospreydirect.co.uk

Photographic credits

Unless otherwise indicated, the author took all the photographs in this work.

Acknowledgements

It is my pleasure to once again showcase the modelling and painting talents of Chris Wauchop in this new title, plus the authentic light and shade of Tom Tullis' profiles. Glenn Irvine's Emil makes a welcome appearance too.

Thanks also to Julie Honey-Simpson of The Russell Group Inc. and, of course, Mr Ed Russell himself for providing access to the immaculate Russell Collection Messerschmitt Bf 109E-4.

This book would not have been possible without the expertise and assistance of a number of individuals who are specialists in their fields. In particular I would like to thank John Beaman, Jerry Crandall, Lynn Ritger, Mark Beckwith, Dominic O'Donnell, Steven Eisenman and Jules Bringuier for their information, advice and opinions over the years. Thanks also to Dr Charles E. Metz and his encyclopedic reference collection.

I am very grateful to Jerry Campbell from Squadron, Dave Klaus from Meteor Productions, David Hannant from Hannants, Gaston Bernal from Aeromaster/Eagle Strike and Kevin McLaughlin from Ultracast for their ongoing enthusiastic support.

And last, but certainly not least, thanks to my wife Debbie and our children, Charlotte and Sebastian, for their continuing indulgence.

Contents

Introduction

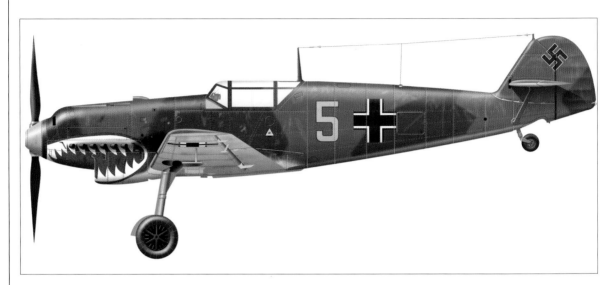

Background

At the outbreak of World War II, Luftwaffe fighters were camouflaged in a low-contrast finish of RLM 70 Black Green and RLM 71 Dark Green on the upper surfaces. This is 'Yellow 5' of 2./JGr 176, based in Germany during August 1939.

By 1940, camouflage had been lightened to suit a more aggressive mode of operation. RLM 02 Grey replaced RLM 70 Black Green as the second upper camouflage colour. The lower surface colour of RLM 65 Light Blue was also brought up the fuselage sides.

The Messerschmitt Bf 109 was built in greater numbers than any other fighter aircraft in history, with over 30,500 Bf 109s produced.

Its service started with the Condor Legion in the Spanish Civil War during the 1930s and it was still in use in Czechoslovakia in the late 1950s under the guise of the Avia S.199. The Spanish postwar Bf 109 powered by the Rolls-Royce Merlin 45 engine, the Buchon HA-1112-M1L, did not retire until 1967. However, the Bf 109 is best known for its role with the Luftwaffe throughout World War II, most famously during the Battle of Britain.

The Bf 109 was an all-metal, low-wing monoplane that signalled the beginning of a new era for fighter aircraft. Willy Messerschmitt's 'Augsburg Eagle' was arguably the best fighter in the world when it entered service in 1937. His design was flexible enough to cope with continual and often dramatic developments over the next seven years.

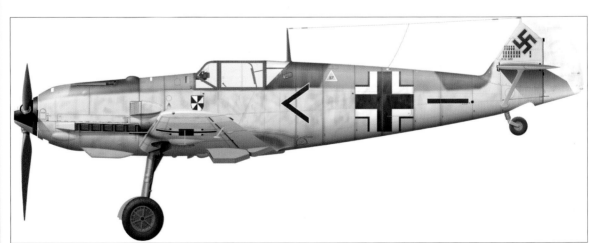

The first Bf 109 variants, equipped with the Jumo 210 engine, were relatively underpowered. Twin machine-gun armament was considered adequate for its day, but would quickly prove to be lacking against a new generation of European fighter aircraft. The adaptable Messerschmitt airframe was transformed with the installation of the Daimler-Benz DB 601 A engine in the Bf 109E-1. Two wing guns were also added during production to supplement the cowl armament.

In this configuration, the Bf 109 was truly ready for war. The new 'Emil' quickly dispatched its adversaries in Poland, the Low Countries and France. When matched against the Royal Air Force, the Bf 109E had the edge on the Hawker Hurricane, Britain's first modern monoplane fighter. In combat with the famous Supermarine Spitfire the odds were closer, with the British design having the upper hand at high altitude. The outcome of each encounter between these legendary thoroughbreds depended on the skill, luck or good eyesight of the pilots involved.

During the course of 1940, the Emil demonstrated its flexibility in the role of fighter-bomber and reconnaissance platform. Performance was further enhanced with the installation of the DB 601N engine, pilot protection improved with windscreen and canopy armour, and firepower increased with the installation of the MG FF/M cannon.

The Messerschmitt Bf 109E soldiered on beyond the Battle of Britain and subsequent Channel skirmishes to participate in campaigns over the Balkans and the Western Desert, Operation *Barbarossa* and even defence of the German homeland against the growing Allied bomber threat.

This book will deal with modelling the Augsburg Eagle from its first variants to the Bf 109E, a period of rapid change in configuration, camouflage and markings.

This Emil demonstrates a higher camouflage demarcation line.

Production variants and characteristics

Conventional wisdom has labelled the earliest production aircraft as the Bf 109B-1, distinguished by the fixed-pitch, wooden Schwarz propeller and inboard-located oil cooler. The later batch is usually referred to as the B-2, having a variable-pitch, metal, two-bladed VDM propeller assembly and the oil cooler relocated outboard of the undercarriage bay.

More recently, however, there has been conjecture that the very first Bf 109s might have been Bf 109A production machines, and that 'B-1' and 'B-2' were never officially adopted terms.

Regardless of the nomenclature, however, it would be fair to say that these earliest Bf 109s underwent a number of noticeable modifications during production and in the field.

For the purpose of this publication, the first production Bf 109s will be called 'Bf 109B early production', with the balance being 'Bf 109B late production'.

The following table lists major production variants.

Table 1: Bf 109 B–E production variants and characteristics

Designation	Characteristics	Comments
Bf 109B early production	Junkers Jumo 210 D engine. Two MG17 cowl-mounted machine guns. Two-bladed fixed-pitch wooden Schwarz propeller. Long wing slats. Oil cooler mounted inboard of landing gear under the port wing. Scissor link on tail gear strut. Exhaust stubs flush with cowl. Cooling slots of various sizes and in different positions were added to the engine cowl panels during production and in the field.	Usually referred to as Bf 109B-1. Some aircraft identified as Bf 109B-1s may have actually been prototypes or Bf 109As. The majority of early production machines were upgraded to late-production standards during their service lives.
Bf 109B late production	As per early production but fitted with variable-pitch, two-bladed metal VDM propeller. Oil cooler moved further outboard under the port wing. Variations observed in position and size of cooling slots.	Usually referred to as Bf 109B-2. Total production of early and late-production machines was 341.
Bf 109C	Junkers Jumo 210 Ga engine fitted for improved high-altitude performance. One MG17 machine gun added to each wing, with corresponding access hatches above and below. Wing slats shortened to accommodate MG17 wing guns. Exhaust stubs protrude from cowl. Oxygen filler and electrical socket on the starboard side of the fuselage moved aft.	55 or 58 produced, depending on the source.
Bf 109D	As above, but reverted back to Jumo 210 D engine. New tail wheel design without scissor link introduced during production.	647 produced. It is sometimes incorrectly reported that the Bf 109D was fitted with the Daimler-Benz DB 600 engine. Some airframe modifications were made in preparation for the new engine, but it was never fitted. Some Bf 109Ds were retrofitted with 109E-style exhausts stacks.
Bf 109E-1	Daimler-Benz DB 601 A engine; three-bladed, variable-pitch metal VDM propeller assembly; completely new nose design to accommodate the new engine; reinforcement strip added above wing root panel. New radiators installed under the wings. Many other minor changes.	1,082 produced. Bf 109E-1s and E-3s were frequently retrofitted with the re-designed canopy and pilot's armour usually associated with the Bf 109E-4. Fighter-bomber variant was also produced (Bf 109E-1/B).
Bf 109E-3	As above, but fitted with one MG FF cannon in each wing. A bulged panel was installed under each wing to allow clearance below the ammunition drum.	1,171 produced. The cannon-armed Bf 109E-3 was not a later development, but was actually produced parallel to the Bf 109E-1. Two prototype Bf 109E-2s were produced with central-firing MG 3/C cannon, but this series was not produced. Fighter-bomber variant was also produced (Bf 109E-3/B)
Bf 109E-4	As above, but standardized with redesigned squared-off canopy and windscreen. New wing armament of MG FF/M with increased rate of fire and improved ammunition. Capacity to carry 300-litre drop tank introduced from November 1940. Horizontal splitter at front of oil cooler housing deleted during production.	Total production uncertain due to rebuilding and upgrade programmes. Sub-variants include Bf 109E-4/B fighter-bomber, Bf 109E-4/N fitted with DB 601N engine (also E-4/N/B), Bf 109E-4/Trop.
Bf 109E-7	As above, but standardized with DB 601N power plant and fittings for a 300-litre drop tank.	429 produced by June 1941. Sub-variants included Bf 109E-7/B fighter-bomber, E-7/Trop (also E-7/B/Trop), Bf 109E-7/U2 ground attack and Bf 109E-7/Z with GM-1 boost
Bf 109E-5, E-6, E-8 and E-9	Reconnaissance fighters.	

Prototypes to Bf 109E in plastic

As one of the most famous fighter aircraft in history, it is not surprising that the Messerschmitt Bf 109 is well represented in plastic.

In the early 1970s, Airfix introduced its spectacular 1/24-scale aircraft models. The Messerschmitt Bf 109E-3/E-4 was one of the first of the series to hit the hobby shop shelves. This kit has been in almost continual release since under either the Airfix or Heller brands. The 1/24-scale Airfix Bf 109E is very accurate in outline. The recessed rivets and engraved panel lines covering the plastic are correctly placed, but are quite heavy and soft. A full engine, gun bays and cockpit are supplied. Detail is good by 1970s standards, but most modellers today would probably want to improve the bare cockpit at a minimum. Ailerons and elevators are hinged, but there is no provision for dropped slats or flaps. The main gear bays are completely featureless, so attention is required here too. Despite these criticisms, however, Airfix's 1/24-scale Bf 109E represents a sound basis for superdetailing, and remains the best large-scale Emil available today.

Later in the same decade, both Hasegawa and Matchbox released 1/32-scale Bf 109E kits. Hasegawa's kit featured fine raised surface features, but suffered a number of outline and detail inaccuracies. The detail on the 1977 Matchbox kit was soft and somewhat simplified, and the deep, trench-like panel lines were distracting, but it was fundamentally an accurate Emil and the better of the two 1/32-scale kits.

Over the years, many Bf 109 kits have been available in 1/72 and 1/48 scale from manufacturers including Airfix, Heller, Minicraft and Monogram. All of these early offerings have been superseded by the more recent generation of Bf 109 kits.

In 1/72 scale, the best Messerschmitt Bf 109s are the E-3/4 kits from ICM and Tamiya. These kits are almost identical in parts layout, but the Tamiya kit fuselage is 2.5mm too short when compared to respected plans. Apart from this problem, Tamiya's kit is perfectly moulded and a joy to build. ICM's fuselage is the correct length, but suffers from soft plastic and some sink marks.

In 1/48 scale, modellers are blessed with a large choice of Emil variants from two manufacturers. Both Tamiya's and Hasegawa's 1/48-scale Messerschmitt Bf 109E kits are excellent. Tamiya's kit is easier to build, while the surface detail on the Hasegawa kit displays more finesse, but there is little to choose between the two. Tamiya offers two kits – a Bf 109E-3 and a Bf 109E-4/7 Trop. Hasegawa

Models of Bf 109 prototypes are rare in any scale. This is HR Model's 1/72-scale Bf 109 V2. The same company also offers a V3 prototype in Spanish Civil War markings.

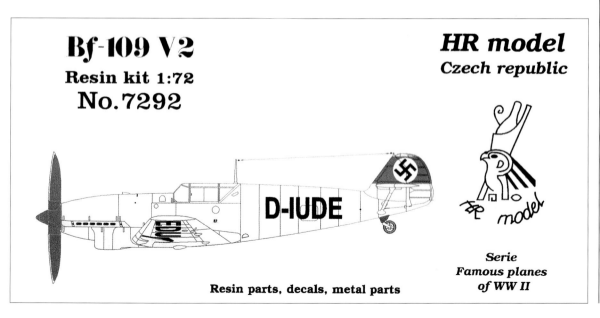

Bf-109 V2

Resin kit 1:72

No. 7292

D-IUDE

Resin parts, decals, metal parts

HR model
Czech republic

Serie
Famous planes
of WW II

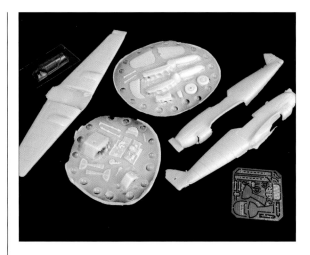

The smaller parts of this kit are cast into a wafer of thin resin. Details are supplied on a photo-etched brass fret.

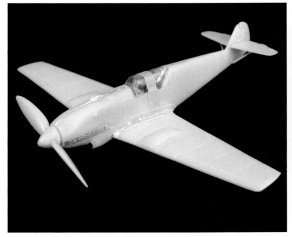

The model conveys the lines of the Bf 109 V2, including unique features of the earliest prototypes. Note the smooth contour of the engine cowl, the large bulges on the tops of the wings and the absence of armament.

Major Helmut Wick's Messerschmitt BF 109E-4. The aircraft displays heavy mottling typical of this unit, apparently applied with a sponge. This is Tamiya's 1/72-scale kit, built and painted by Glenn Irvine.

has released at least 19 variations on the Emil theme since 1993, including the Bf 109E-1, E-3, E-4 E-7, Trop and T-1.

The choice of Jumo-powered Bf 109s is more limited in both popular scales. The old 1/72-scale Heller Bf 109D is not a bad little kit. It is accurate in outline and features fine raised panel lines, but offers only basic details. AML's more recent 1/72-scale Bf 109D is a multimedia affair with resin cockpit, a large photo-etched fret and a colourful decal sheet. However, the limited run nature of this kit means that it cannot be recommended to beginners.

Hobbycraft offered a series of 1/48-scale Bf 109B/C/D kits in the early 1990s. Their Bf 109D is still available under the Academy brand. These are simple models, easy to build but with a number of accuracy problems. Classic Airframes is due to launch their family of Bf 109 prototypes and Jumo-powered production variants around the time this book will be published.

Options for building the prototypes are even more limited, with HR Models' 1/72-scale Bf 109 V2 and V3 resin models being the only kits currently available.

Table 2: Messerschmitt Bf 109 Prototype to E kits in 1/72, 1/48, 1/32 and 1/24 scales

Brand	Item number	Description	Comments
1/72 scale			
A Model	7205	Messerschmitt Bf 109E	
A Model	72116	Messerschmitt Bf 109E-3 Romanian Aces	
A Model	72117	Messerschmitt Bf 109E-3/E-4	
Academy	2133	Messerschmitt Bf 109E	
Academy	2214	Messerschmitt Bf 109E with Kubelwagen	
Airfix	2048	Messerschmitt Bf 109E	
AML	7208	Messerschmitt Bf 109D with etched parts	
AML	7228	Messerschmitt Bf 109D UPGRADE with resin	
Heller	8026	Messerschmitt Bf 109D	Not in current release
HR Models	7292	Messerschmitt Bf 109V2	Resin kit
HR Models	7294	Messerschmitt Bf 109V3 Legion Condor	Resin kit
ICM	72131	Messerschmitt Bf 109E-3	
ICM	72132	Messerschmitt Bf 109E-4	
MPM	72132	Messerschmitt Bf 109T UPGRADED	
Seminar	1472	Messerschmitt Bf 109E-4	
Tamiya	60750	Messerschmitt Bf 109E-3	
Tamiya	60755	Messerschmitt Bf 109E-4/7Tropical	
1/48 scale			
Academy	2178	Messerschmitt Bf 109D	Ex-Hobbycraft with all options
Classic Airframes	4123	Messerschmitt Bf 109 early	Prototypes and 109B
Hasegawa	9563	Messerschmitt Bf 109E-7 Balkan Theatre	
Hasegawa	9601	Messerschmitt Bf 109E-3 'Spanish Civil War'	
Hasegawa	9624	Messerschmitt Bf 109E3 "Romanian Air Force"	
Hasegawa	9643	Messerschmitt Bf 109E-4/7 Trop.	
Hasegawa	9671	Messerschmitt Bf 109E-4 'Wick'	
MPM	48023	Messerschmitt Bf 109T-1/2	
MPM	48043	Messerschmitt Bf 109T UPGRADE with resin	
Revell	4572	Messerschmitt Bf 109E-4/7	Ex-Hasegawa. No photoetch
Tamiya	61050	Messerschmitt Bf 109E-3	
Tamiya	61063	Messerschmitt Bf 109E-4/7	
1/32 scale			
Hasegawa	T001	Messerschmitt Bf 109E	
Matchbox	PK502	Messerschmitt Bf 109E	Not in current release
1/24 scale			
Airfix	12002	Messerschmitt Bf 109	Also released by Heller

The Messerschmitt Bf 109E-4 in detail

This chapter contains images of an immaculately restored Messerschmitt Bf 109E-4, W.Nr 3579 'White 14', owned by Mr Ed Russell and hangared near Niagara in Canada.

This beautifully restored Messerschmitt Bf 109E-4, W.Nr 3579 is owned by Mr Ed Russell. It is finished in the Battle of Britain markings of Hans Joachim Marseille.

The cockpit is remarkably authentic for a fully operational warbird. The main departures from the World War II original are the missing gunsight at the top of the instrument panel and the modern radio at the bottom left. Some of the engine instruments (at the bottom of the panel) seem to have been replaced with more modern counterparts too.

The timber-lined trim wheel is of interest. Some English-language labels have been added to assist the modern pilots of this rare warbird.

The starboard cockpit sidewall is also authentic, but the original paint finish would have been flat, not glossy as seen here. The high gloss surface is more durable and highlights damage more easily than the flat wartime paint.

The fuse panel, underneath the starboard side quarter window, features English labels. Also note the ultraviolet instrument light immediately above the fuse panel.

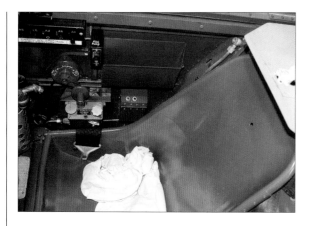

The one-piece bucket seat of the Bf 109E was quite different to that found in later variants.

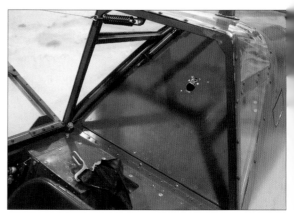

The pilot had a stowage compartment behind the cockpit.

A hinged door opens to permit small items to be stowed. This is also a good view of the canopy-retaining wire and its spring, secured to the rear canopy section.

The opening section of the canopy features sliding windows on the top and on each side.

These windows can be slid open by a small knob glued to the plexiglass. The crank on the bottom frame is the canopy-release lever.

Note that there is no hard frame between the two clear sliding panels.

The windscreen side sections on the Bf 109E often had a small opening quarter window, although it is not fitted to this restored example.

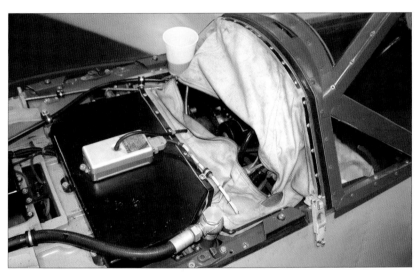

A zippered canvas cover protects the rear of the instrument panel from the grime of the engine bay, as well as cordite stains and smoke from the cowl machine guns.

The cowl machine guns are not fitted, but their mounts and the interrupter mechanism may be seen in this view.

The machine-gun troughs on the Bf 109E were a deep, tapered oval shape pressed into the metal of a separate panel. The outline of the gun trough panel may be seen here.

The radiator intake and latch detail may be seen in this view.

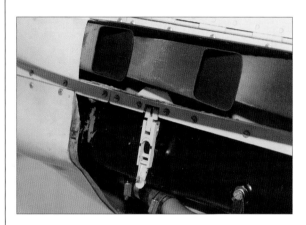

Exhaust stacks are almost square in profile. Each stack also features a lengthwise raised seam running along the centreline, front to rear, although they are not very obvious in this photo!

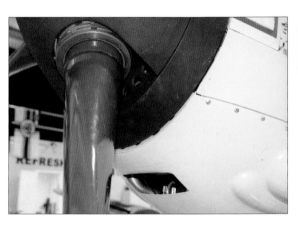

The spinner backplate features a myriad of ventilation holes, some of which may just be seen behind the propeller blade in this photo. The unpainted pitch collar is also visible at the base of the blade.

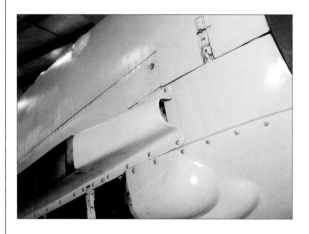

The shroud at the front of the exhaust assembly is open at the face. Note the various bulges on the bottom corner of the cowl to accommodate the front of the cylinder heads and engine plumbing.

Hydraulics, piping and electrical wiring create quite a colourful jumble at the bottom of the engine bay.

This view is underneath the fuselage, from the back of the engine bay looking aft. Note the substantial frame structure under the cockpit, and the large fuel tank (painted green to the rear) strapped in behind the vertical bulkhead.

The octane rating of 87 is noted on a stencil just below the main fuel filler access hatch on the fuselage spine.

Isolators on the antenna wire are protected by small, aerodynamic fairings. The wire itself is simply hooked to the small mast on the fin.

Elevator trim is achieved via a movable horizontal stabilizer. Take-off trim position is indicated by the '0', while maximum deflection is marked at the top and the bottom of the slot. A large wheel in the cockpit controls the trim position.

Control surfaces are fabric covered. While the rest of the airframe is glossy, these surfaces are dead flat. Ribbing tape is also obvious in this view.

The non-retracting, castoring tail wheel may be locked for take off.

Rudder control is achieved via actuator rods that protrude from the rear fuselage.

The bulge in the wing root fairing covers a large locking bolt. Also note the prominent reinforcement strip at the top of the wing root fairing. This feature was introduced with the E model.

The MG FF wing machine gun projects beyond the leading edge. Note the relatively large opening surrounding the barrel.

Leading edge slats improve lift at low speed by 'squeezing' air over the top of the wing. The slats are mechanically operated, deploying automatically at low speeds.

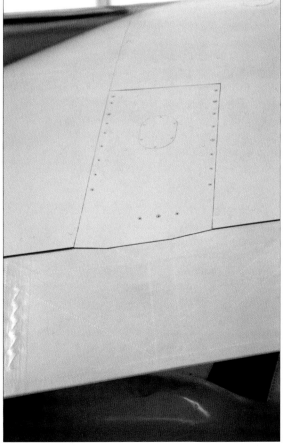

The different rates of fading and variation in colour between metal and fabric surfaces are very obvious in this view. The large rectangular panel is the access hatch for the wing-mounted MG FF machine gun.

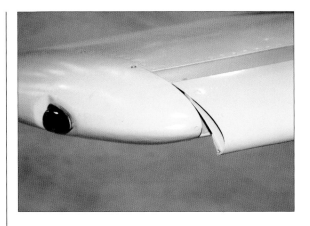

Detail of the starboard side wing tip. Note the hollow end of the slat, and how it deploys down and out. The wing-tip navigation light would have been green on the wartime aircraft.

Detail view of the starboard elevator (on the right) and the landing flap. Both of these control surfaces are covered with fabric.

Each wing radiator housing is reinforced with a vertical brace at its face. Note the ventilation flap at the rear too, flopped open in this photo.

The pitot tube is usually covered when the aircraft is parked to avoid dirt and dust clogging this sensitive instrument.

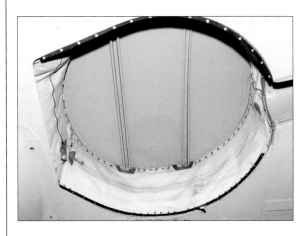

The wheel wells of the Messerschmitt Bf 109E were often fitted with a removable canvas cover. The main wheels kicked up a lot of dirt. These covers protected the interior of the wing from this debris.

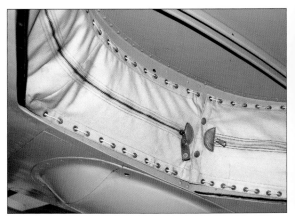

The prominent stitching at the top and bottom is very clear here. Zippers around the middle of the covers permit easy inspection of the wing interior.

The port-side gear leg of the Messerschmitt Bf 109E. Note the hydraulic line running down the front of the leg, held in place with two metal restraining straps. The bottom of the hydraulic line is made of a flexible material and looped to take into account the altering heights of the oleo strut depending on load.

The cast-metal main wheel is painted gloss black, in common with its wartime counterparts.

First in combat – Berta in Spain

Subject:	Messerschmitt Bf 109B early production
Modeller:	Brett Green
Skill level:	Master
Base kit:	Academy (Hobbycraft) Bf 109D; Revell (Hasegawa) Bf 109E-4/7/Trop
Scale:	1/32
Additional detailing sets used:	True Details resin cockpit; True Details resin wheels; resin propeller from Classic Airframes Hurricane Mk I; various plastic and metal strip, sheet and scrap
Paints:	Alclad
Markings:	Various markings from Cutting Edge Decal sheets

Hobbycraft's 1/48-scale Bf 109B/C/D kits in the box

Hobbycraft first released their family of 1/48-scale early Messerschmitt Bf 109 kits around 1992. This was the first time that the Jumo-powered Bf 109 variants had been offered in 1/48 scale by a mainstream manufacturer.

Some years earlier, Falcon of New Zealand released a vacuum-formed kit, and later also produced a limited-run injection-moulded model of the Bf 109B. Both these kits were accurate, but required a reasonable amount of effort in preparation and sourcing of detail parts. The modelling community therefore warmly welcomed Hobbycraft's sleek injection-moulded kits.

Hobbycraft released Bf 109B, C and D kits in quick succession. These models each contained around 43 parts in crisp grey plastic. Each model offered different options for the particular variants. For example, the Bf 109B kit included the fixed-pitch wooden Schwarz propeller, and different styles of exhausts were supplied with each kit. The latter feature was somewhat odd, as there were only really two styles of exhaust.

These kits were inexpensive upon release, and can still be picked up cheaply in the dark recesses of hobby shop shelves and at swap meets.

In 1999, Academy re-packaged Hobbycraft's Bf 109D. This kit included all the options previously spread amongst the three Hobbycraft releases, and Academy's decals were a great improvement over the originals. The Academy Bf 109D kit is still on general release.

The outline of Hobbycraft's early 109s is basically correct, and the kits offer some attractive features. These include crisply recessed panel lines, optional position landing flaps and a nicely detailed cockpit.

However, closer inspection of the kit reveals a number of shortcomings. There are some shape problems around the forward fuselage and the tail. Much of the detail moulded to the nose – vents, panel lines, gun troughs – is incorrectly positioned or missing. The stabilizer struts are too long to use without modification. The fuselage side features a raised reinforcement strip above the wing root fairing that was actually introduced with the Bf 109E. The one-piece canopy makes an open cockpit display difficult, and it looks generally undersized. The cockpit configuration is more typical of a Bf 109E than an early 109. Finally, the Schwarz propeller included for the early production 109B does have two fixed blades, but otherwise bears little resemblance to the real thing.

Armed with this long list of niggling issues, I was faced with a decision. Do I grit my teeth and tolerate the errors, or do I try to fix them?

Kitbashing a better Berta

The biggest distinguishing feature of the early Bf 109 variants was its nose. The forward fuselage was a completely different shape from the Emil, due to the installation of the Jumo 210 power plant. Other differences included the two-bladed propeller and lack of wing armament in the early Bf 109B.

Even so, the 109B/C/D and E shared a lot in common. I wondered if it might be possible to graft the nose of the Hobbycraft kit onto the much better fuselage and wings of Hasegawa's Bf 109E. This would be a good way to avoid a number of the problems with Hobbycraft's kit.

Only one way to find out.

First I selected the donor kits. I wanted to depict an early Bf 109B, so I needed a model with the Schwarz propeller. I purchased the Academy Bf 109D, which offered this option. Revell's re-boxing of Hasegawa's Bf 109E-4/7/Trop was chosen for the back half of this hybrid. Revell's offering is less expensive than Hasegawa's version, but it is missing the photo-etched parts included in the Hasegawa kits. This is a problem if you are actually building an Emil, as you will need to scratch build canopy armour and radiator grilles. It is not a problem with this project, however, as early Bf 109s were not fitted with these features.

Now, where is that razor saw?

Initial inspection suggested that this mating should work. I decided to cut the Hobbycraft nose off in a staggered line, with the upper demarcation being at the rearmost engine cover panel, and behind the radiator at the bottom of the nose. The equivalent section of Hasegawa's kit nose was also cut off.

Upon test fitting, I was relieved to find that the cross sections of the kits matched surprisingly well at the join. Poor alignment at the fuselage join was by far the biggest risk of this kitbash.

Hobbycraft's nose and Hasegawa's fuselage segments were glued together as separate halves then compared to published drawings. The overall length appeared to be a few millimetres short when laid over the plans, so the newly joined hybrid was carefully separated. A spacer of plastic strip was glued behind the join on each main fuselage half, then the nose sections were re-assembled a few millimetres forward of their original position to deliver the correct length.

The Messerschmitt Bf 109 was first tested under fire during the Spanish Civil War. This is an early production Messerschmitt Bf 109B, featuring the two-bladed, fixed-pitch wooden Schwarz propeller, long leading edge slats and armed with just two rifle-calibre machine guns.

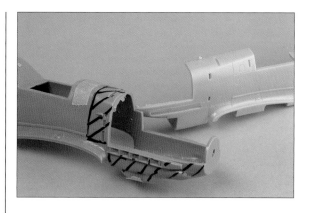

Kitbash! In the absence of a really good early Bf 109 kit in 1/48 scale at the time of writing, the Hobbycraft and Hasegawa kits were combined for this project. Kit parts were compared to plans then carefully cut as the first step of this cosmetic surgery.

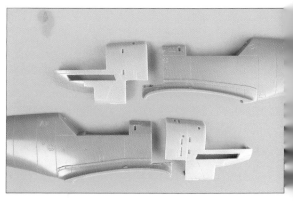

The light grey parts are from Hobbycraft's Bf 109B, while the medium grey rear fuselage is Hasegawa's Bf 109E-3.

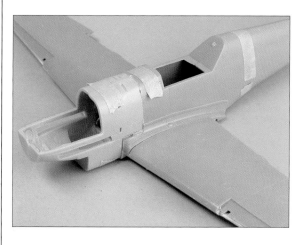

When the combined parts were laid down on plans, the overall fuselage length was a few millimetres too short.

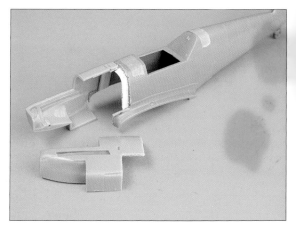

The Hobbycraft and Hasegawa parts were carefully disassembled, and a spacer of plastic strip was glued between the parts.

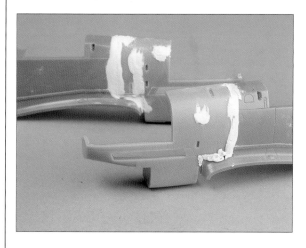

The resulting gap between the Hobbycraft nose and the Hasegawa mid fuselage was filled using Milliput two-part epoxy putty.

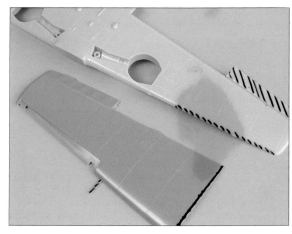

Hasegawa's upper wing halves combined with Hobbycraft's lower wing. Ailerons and leading edge slats were carefully cut from the Hobbycraft lower wings as indicated in this photograph.

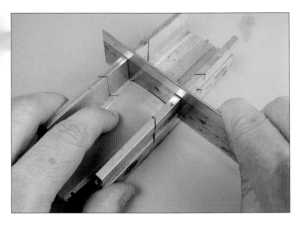

Test fitting suggested that Hasegawa's upper wing halves would foul at the wing roots. Less than 2mm was sawn off the inboard section of each wing.

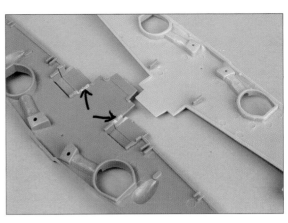

Support braces inboard of the wing radiators (the position of which are indicated here by the arrows) were cut from Hasegawa's lower wing and glued in the same position on Hobbycraft's wing. This lent structural integrity to the new hybrid wing.

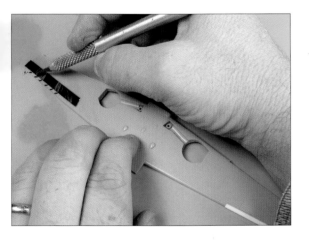

Further trimming and shimming was required before Hasegawa's ailerons would fit with Hobbycraft's lower wing.

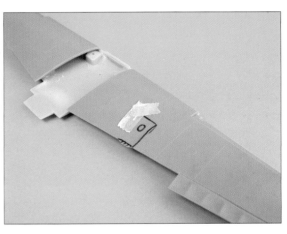

Gun access panels on Hasegawa's upper wing were masked, filled and sanded flat. These were not present on the earliest 109s.

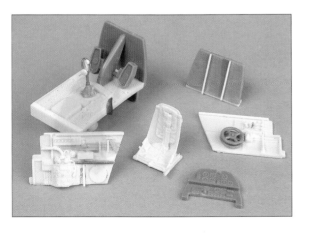

True Details' 1/48-scale resin cockpit, item number TD49005, was adapted to represent a 109B front office. The oval-shaped control yoke and modified starboard sidewalls are noteworthy.

Early 109 cockpits were finished in RLM 02 Grey. The resin parts were sprayed, then received a wash of thinned burnt umber oil paint before the final details were picked out with a fine brush.

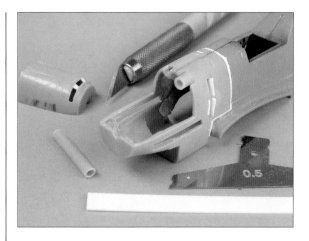

Gun troughs and cooling slots represented the biggest challenge for this project. Hobbycraft's gun troughs were deepened and lengthened with the assistance of Contrail styrene tube.

Significant amounts of putty – in this case Milliput – were essential to fill gaps and smooth contours of the hybrid nose. Also note the rebuilt large cooling slots in the front of the nose.

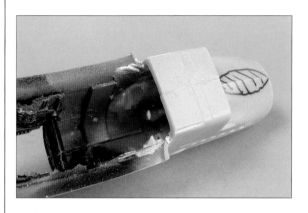

Hobbycraft's lower nose features a peculiar 'turkey neck', as indicated by the red ink. This was sanded to a smooth curve.

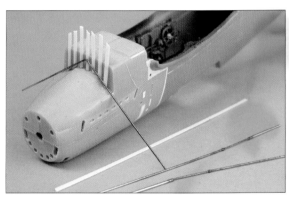

Radiator face and brace detail was added using styrene strip and fine brass rod. These long sections were cut to the correct length when they had set.

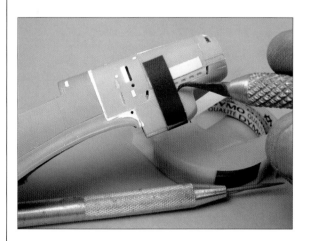

With the basic shape of the nose completed, it was time to replace panel line detail. Self-adhesive Dymo tape was used as a guide to scribe these lines.

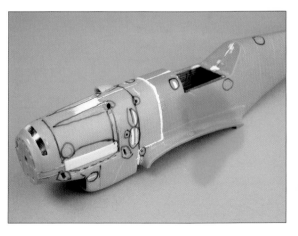

The red ink indicated surface features than have been filled or otherwise eliminated. The blue ink shows new or relocated panel lines, cooling slots and other features.

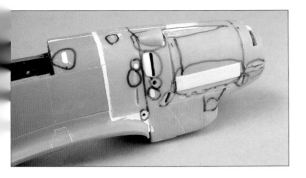

The large intake scoop was relocated rearward. Scrap plastic was employed for the access panel above the exhausts. Note that the raised reinforcement strip above the wing root fairing has also been sanded smooth.

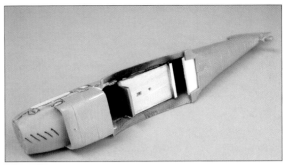

The resin cockpit tub was fitted after the fuselage was completed. A wedge of plastic was installed where the centre wing would meet the lower fuselage to reinforce this important join.

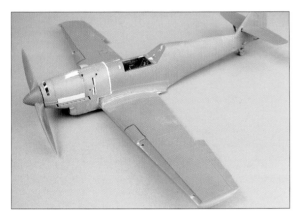

After the main components were assembled, I realized that this aircraft featured long-span slats. The wider slat position was marked and cut out of the assembled wings – not the easiest construction sequence!

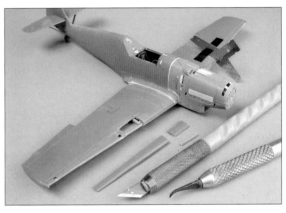

The surgery was conducted very carefully because I wanted to use the section of upper wing to extend the Hasegawa kit slats. The vertical cut was first, using a photo-etched razor saw. The section was then sliced out using a scriber followed by a new hobby blade.

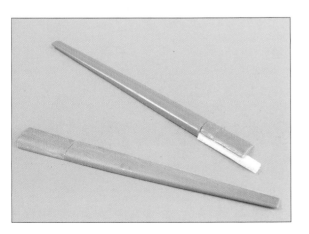

The excised upper wing leading edge section was glued to the Hasegawa slats, then filled and sanded smooth.

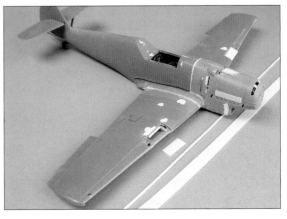

The resulting openings in the wing leading edges were blanked off with strip plastic. Various access hatches in the upper wing, not applicable to the Bf 109B, were filled with Liquid Paper and sanded flat.

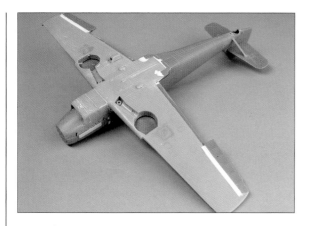

A little more filling was required where the centre of the wing meets the lower fuselage, but fit was otherwise good.

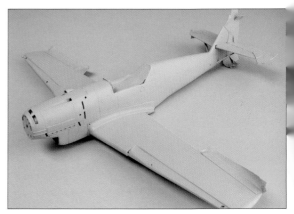

A coat of Tamiya Primer was helpful on two counts. First, it was a good way to check for misaligned panel lines and gaps. Secondly, it was an essential base coat for the coming metallic lacquer.

The model received several thin overall coats of Alclad II Aluminum Shade A lacquer.

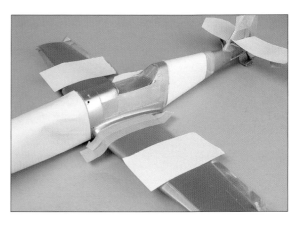

Selected panels were masked before a darker shade was sprayed.

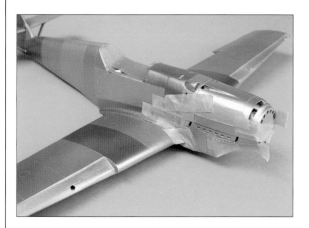

Two more metallic shades were applied to other panels. This technique replicates the uneven finish noted on the earliest Bertas deployed in Spain.

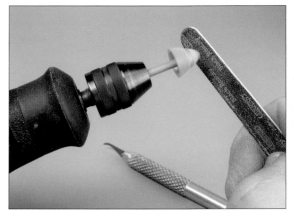

I was not happy with the shape of Hobbycraft's Schwarz prop assembly. Instead, I started with the Watts propeller in Classic Aiframes' fabric-wing Hurricane kit. The spinner was glued to a piece of sprue and mounted in my Dremel motor tool.

The shape of the spinner was made more blunt by selective sanding, and panel lines were carefully scribed in place. The propeller blades were reshaped too.

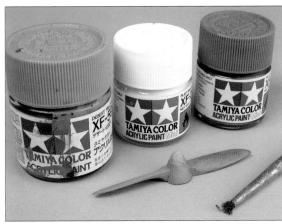

The blades were painted to represent wood. A base coat of Tamiya Desert Yellow was given a grain using drybrushed Earth Brown and Flat White

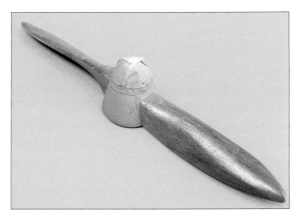

The woodgrain blades were then coated with Future floor polish.

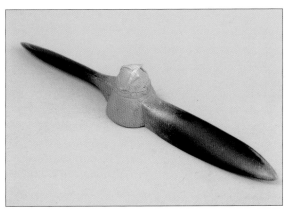

Next, the blades were sprayed flat black and sanded back to the woodgrain at the tips and bases of the propeller blades. This pattern of weathering may be seen in wartime photos.

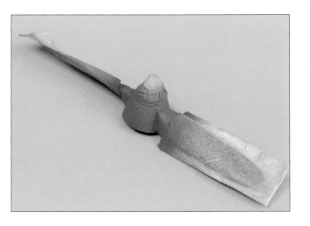

The colours of the spinner are anybody's guess. I painted the base of the spinner RLM 02 Grey.

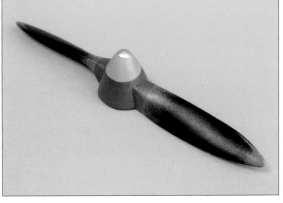

The front of the spinner was painted yellow, possibly a *Staffel* identification colour. The tip of the spinner was capped with a circle of self-adhesive aluminium foil.

The small gaps in the leading edge of the flaps were filled, and locating pins were added from steel wire. The tail wheel was also modified. Oleo scissors came from a 1/72-scale photo-etched fret.

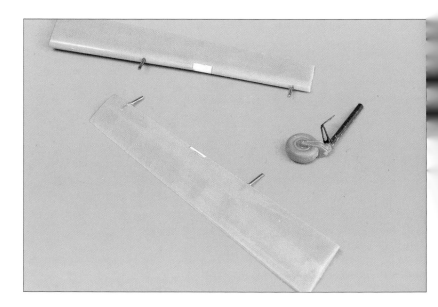

The resulting gap between the Hobbycraft nose and Hasegawa mid-fuselage was filled using Milliput two-part epoxy putty.

An added benefit of this kitbash is the opportunity to use Hasegawa's upper wings and their separate slats. I decided to use Hobbycraft's lower wings, however, as the forward cross section matches perfectly with Hobbycraft's nose, and there are no lower wing bulges to be removed.

The moulded-on ailerons and slats were carefully cut from Hobbycraft's full-span lower wing. The panel lines were first deepened with a scriber to minimize the risky work associated with the sharp hobby knife. The newly prepared lower wing was test fitted to the upper wing halves, then offered to the fuselage halves. A few millimetres had to be shaved from the Hasegawa wing parts at the wing root to ensure a good fit.

Before the wing was assembled, braces were installed to prop the top wing halves up to assist alignment with the fuselage wing root. A little more fiddling and trimming, especially around the ailerons, was required before the wings were assembled.

The earliest Bf 109s were not fitted with wing guns, so the access panels on the top of Hasegawa's wing halves were filled and sanded flat. The overhanging back of each cannon access hatch was also cut off flush with the wing trailing edge.

With the wings set aside to dry, it was time to consider the front office. True Details' Bf 109E cockpit is inexpensive but nicely detailed. The resin parts were modified to represent an early Berta. A Bf 109B captured by the Republicans during the Spanish Civil War was photographed extensively, including the cockpit area. These images show a fairly bare starboard sidewall. This may have been an early cockpit configuration, or it may simply be that the map case was removed before the photo was taken. Regardless, I decided that my cockpit would be modified to match the photos. I achieved this by slicing the cast-on map case from the starboard sidewall and adding structural detail from strip and scrap plastic.

Another difference between this and later cockpits is the oval-shaped control yoke, more reminiscent of a Spitfire than a 109. A new control column was fashioned from putty, plastic and fuse wire. With the main cockpit subassemblies completed, the sidewalls were glued to the inside of the fuselage and painting commenced.

The pale RLM 02 Grey colour really shows off the detail of the 109's front office. A wash of thinned burnt umber oil paint further emphasized the shadows of the cockpit's recesses before small details were picked out with acrylic paint and a fine brush.

The fuselage halves were now joined, and some of the hardest work began. In addition to reference photos, I found Lynn Ritger's online article on correcting the Hobbycraft kit nose very helpful at this stage. This article may be found on 'The 109 Lair' at http://109lair.hobbyvista.com/index1024.htm.

Attention was now turned to the undersized gun troughs. Not only are these too shallow and narrow, but they also do not extend anywhere near far enough back. I cut slots behind the engine cowl, and installed short lengths of Contrail plastic tube. Once they were glued in place along their centreline, the top halves were sliced off, resulting in two nice, neat trough extensions with semicircular cross section.

Before the top engine cowl was glued in place, the forward sections of the gun troughs were widened and deepened with a rat-tail file to match the cross sections of the trough extensions. A noticeable step was present at the top rear of the engine cowl when the part was installed. Milliput, a slow-curing two-part epoxy putty, was used to fill the step and smooth the contours of the upper nose and engine cowling.

Cooling slots were filled and/or repositioned as required. I initially had a great deal of trouble cutting straight, clean slots in the sides of the nose. I eventually cut oversized slots, and packed each side with plastic strip to achieve the correct width for the narrow openings. When the glue had dried, the protruding plastic strip was cut flush with the plastic of the kit parts and any remaining gaps were filled and sanded flat.

The lower nose in front of the radiator features a peculiar dangling 'turkey neck'. This was quickly and easily sanded to a smooth curve. The radiator itself is a bit too squared off in cross-section, and lacks interior detail. I decided I could live with the shape, but I did add face and brace structures using plastic strip and fine brass rod.

Decals were sourced from two Cutting Edge sets. They performed flawlessly over the metallic finish.

With the nose shapes and structural details completed, new panel lines were scribed using self-adhesive Dymo tape as a guide. The last tasks in this area were the relocation rearward of the carburettor intake scoop (easy, as it is supplied as a separate part), and the addition of a raised strip – spark plug access panels I believe – above the exhausts.

The cockpit tub was installed in the fuselage and secured with a bead of superglue. It was very satisfying to finally mate the fuselage and wings. The model was really taking shape.

Just as I was preparing to rest on my laurels, I noticed a detail I had previously missed in photos. The aircraft I wanted to depict was fitted with long slats! In the first instance I thought, hey, who is going to notice? This thought did not linger long. I therefore set about the risky task of slicing open the assembled wing. The surgery was all the more delicate because I wanted to use the excised sections of wing as the extension for the slats. Great care was required to avoid damaging the plastic.

Time and care resulted in an acceptable result. The kit slats were glued to the slat extensions. The new openings in the leading edge of the wings were blanked off with plastic card and sanded smooth. Although it worked out okay this time around, I do not recommend this sequence of construction! If you want to depict long slats, it will be much easier to do so before the wing is assembled.

A number of small panels on the wing were filled, as was the spine-mounted fuel access hatch on the fuselage. A round fuel filler point was scribed underneath the cockpit, appropriate to this variant. The raised strip above the wing root fairing was also sanded off each side of the fuselage.

Considering the hybrid nature of this project, overall fit was remarkably good. Some filler was required at the lower wing and fuselage join, but there were few other areas that required attention.

Painting

With all the cross-kitting and re-scribing, it was important to check that there were no rogue gaps, scratches or misalignment. Any flaws would be instantly emphasized by the metallic Alclad coat that the model was destined to wear. Tamiya Grey Primer was sprayed onto the model straight from the can. This provided an even surface to check for errors and an essential base for the following Alclad.

The grey primer coat was buffed to a high shine with Micro-Mesh polishing cloths, starting with 3,600 grade and working up to 12,000 grade. This was followed by several thin coats of Alclad II Aluminium 'Shade A' acrylic lacquer. The model was masked and received several additional layers of different Alclad shades. The steel engine-inspection panel, as well as the surrounds of the radiator core and exhausts, were masked last and sprayed Tamiya XF-1 Flat Black.

Decals were sourced from two Cutting Edge decal sheets. The shiny Alclad finish did not require any further gloss coat prior to application of the decals. The markings behaved beautifully, conforming instantly to panel lines and other surface features.

The first batch of Bf 109s sent to Spain was long believed to have worn an overall finish of light grey or RLM 02 Grey. However, in his recent book *Luftwaffe Camouflage and Markings 1933–1945 Volume One*, Ken Merrick suggests that these very early Legion Condor Bf 109s were apparently finished in a very thin coat of a colour similar to RLM 02. This transparent coat permitted the irregularities of the bare metal to show clearly through, but resulted in a greenish tinge to the surface.

I did try to replicate this green tinge using several methods, but I was unhappy with all of them. In the end, I decided to simply apply a flat finish. Next time, I will add a small amount of RLM 02 paint to the Alclad *before* spraying.

Finally, the model was weathered with a thin mix of Tamiya XF-1 Flat Black and XF-64 Red Brown sprayed along panel lines and as a light exhaust stain.

ABOVE The hybrid kit conveys the attractive lines of Willy
Messerschmitt's early fighter design.

BELOW Panel lines were weathered with a thin mix of Tamiya
XF-1 Flat Black and XF-64 Red Brown.

ABOVE The earliest Bf 109s in Spain were delivered in bare metal with a protective coat of translucent zinc chromate, which displayed the irregularities of the metal beneath.

BELOW Hasegawa's fuselage, upper wings and canopy are a vast improvement over Hobbycraft's counterparts.

ABOVE The overall shape of the kit is accurate, and unique attributes of the earliest Bf 109s, including long slats and the wooden Schwarz propeller assembly, are all represented.

BELOW Classic Airframes released its 1/48-scale early Bf 109 kit in January 2006. This brand new model offers the option to build the Bf 109 V4, V5, A or B straight from the box.

ABOVE Classic Airframes' model also features separate control surfaces, permitting dropped slats, flaps, elevators and deflected ailerons if desired.

BELOW Resin and photo-etched parts combine with the high-quality plastic to make Classic Airframes' new offering easily the best Jumo-powered Bf 109 model currently available in any scale.

Phoney war Emil

Subject:	*Messerschmitt Bf 109E-1*
Modeller:	*Brett Green*
Skill level:	*Moderate*
Base kit:	*Hobbycraft Bf 109E-3*
Scale:	*1/48*
Additional detailing sets used:	*'Prop Blur' photo-etched propeller; pilot from Tamiya Bf 109E-4; Metal rod and plastic base*
Paints:	*Gunze acrylics using a Testor Aztek A470 airbrush*
Markings:	*Various markings from the spares box*

Hobbycraft 1/48-scale Messerschmitt Bf 109E-1, E-3 and E-4/7 kits in the box

Hobbycraft released the first in their family of 1/48-scale Emils in 1992. Hasegawa already had several Bf 109E kits on the market at this stage, but these early offerings displayed noticeable inaccuracies around the forward fuselage. By comparison, Hobbycraft's new kits did not look too bad.

Hobbycraft's 1/48-scale Bf 109E-3 and E-4 kits featured crisp, finely recessed panel lines, optional position flaps as separate parts, a reasonable level of detail, especially in the cockpit, and good fit. A nice selection of ordnance was also supplied in the form of drop tanks and bombs.

On the down side, the nose had a bloated overall appearance with a number of fictitious bulges on the top corners. The tail section was also not quite right, the stabilizers did not reach far enough forward to pass through the slot in the front of the fin, the stabilizer struts were too long, radiators were not blanked off, resulting in a see-through effect, and the one-piece canopy made life difficult for modellers who wanted to display an open cockpit.

Hasegawa delivered a body blow to Hobbycraft when it launched a newly tooled and much more accurate series of Bf 109E kits in 1993. Hobbycraft's offerings were now clearly surpassed by Hasegawa in terms of accuracy, detail and finesse.

Hobbycraft only maintained the high ground in two areas. Their Emils were inexpensive, and the separate lower wing cannon bulges made conversion to a Bf 109E-1 quite simple.

Putting Hobbycraft's Emil to flight

I started building Hobbycraft's Bf 109E-3 way back in 1993. I was satisfied with the level of cockpit detail and construction of the simple model proceeded quickly.

By the time I had assembled the fuselage and the wings, Hasegawa had released the first of their re-tooled Bf 109E kits. I took one look at Hasegawa's improved offering and my enthusiasm for Hobbycraft's kit quickly cooled.

The model was tossed back in the box and remained there for nearly 12 years.

When I was gathering kits for this book, I came across the half forgotten, dusty Hobbycraft box. The model was intact – a plastic time capsule from the early 1990s. I actually felt a little guilty that I had abandoned this project at such an advanced stage, so I decided to resurrect the kit and finish this Emil.

Hobbycraft 1/48-scale Messerschmitt Bf 109E-1, E-3 and E-4/7 kits

Pros
- Crisp, appropriate and restrained surface details (panel lines, recessed rivets and subtly raised fabric texture)
- Choice of dropped or raised flaps
- Optional ordnance (bombs, racks)
- Good fit
- Reasonable level of detail
- Simple conversion to Bf 109E-1
- Available inexpensively

Cons
- Outline accuracy problems around nose and tail
- One-piece canopy (undersized in E-3 kit)
- Stabilizer struts too long
- No option for dropped slats
- See-through radiators
- Surpassed in virtually all respects by latest mouldings from Hasegawa and Tamiya

A Messerschmitt Bf 109E-1 of II/JG 53, 'Pik As', in flight over Germany toward the end of 1939. This *Geschwader* employed some interesting experimental camouflage during the period of the Phoney War.

The lack of lower cannon bulges made the variant an easy choice. This would be finished as a Bf 109E-1. The aircraft would be depicted in-flight too. That way I would not have to slice open the one-piece canopy.

The first task after my 12-year intermission was to glue the upper cowl in place. This part appeared to be slightly warped, not aligning properly with the fuselage sides and the nose. Plastic clamps were used to force the cowl into the correct position before liquid glue was flowed into the join lines.

I was not pleased with the flat dihedral of the wings. I scribed the upper wing roots to separate the wings from the fuselage, then stretched Tamiya masking tape from wing tip to wing tip, adjusting until a more appropriate dihedral was achieved. Liquid glue was then brushed generously into the wing root to fix this angle permanently.

In my eagerness to finish this project back in 1993, I had not addressed the open radiator fairings. With the benefit of hindsight I should have blanked off the radiators with a strip of plastic card before the wing halves were joined.

Because the model was destined to be displayed in flight, the flaps needed to be glued in the 'up' position. The fit of Hobbycraft's flaps was awful. They were obviously intended to be glued in the 'down' position. I test fitted a spare set of Hasegawa flaps, which fitted marginally better than the kit parts.

With the wings and fuselage now assembled, it was time to sit back and admire my handiwork. The more I stared at the model, the worse the forward fuselage looked. I almost tossed the Emil into its box for another 12 years of storage before I eventually bit the bullet and decided to see if I could improve the nose profiles.

Armed with a coarse sanding stick I recontoured the nose, slimming the forward fuselage sides and removing the odd, fictitious bulges from the top corners. Apart from the overblown appearance, there is also insufficient slope from the windscreen to the tip of the nose. The sanding stick was also used to

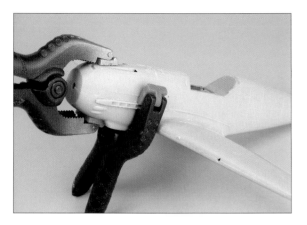

The fit of Hobbycraft's 1/48-scale Bf 109E kit is reasonable, but the separate top cowl does present some challenges. Plastic clamps are being used to align the parts until the glue has dried.

Tamiya masking tape is stretched from wingtip to wingtip to improve the dihedral, which is almost flat without assistance.

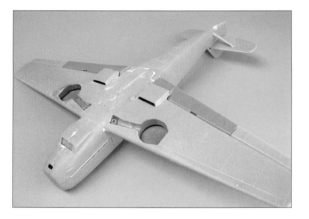

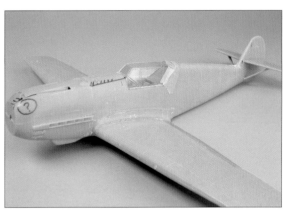

One benefit of the Hobbycraft kit is that the lower-wing cannon bulges are separate parts. This makes it simpler to build the E-1 variant, which was not equipped with cannon.

Hobbycraft's forward fuselage is bloated and oversimplified. Amongst other sins, the nose lacks a downward slope from the windscreen, and includes fictitious bulges at the top front corners.

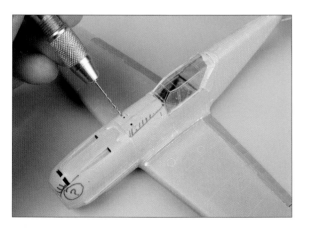

Ventilation slots were cut out in preparation for a nose job.

Hobbycraft's plastic was recontoured with a coarse sanding stick, slimming the forward fuselage sides and creating a shallow slope to the front of the nose.

Not perfect by any means, but an improvement over the original shape.

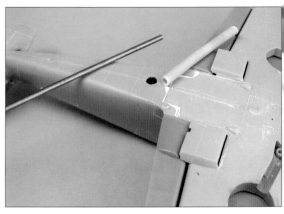

This model was destined to be mounted on a stand. A hole was drilled into the bottom of the fuselage.

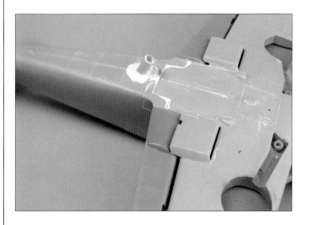

A section of plastic tube was glued into the hole, then puttied to eliminate any gaps. The overhanging length was sliced off flush with the bottom of the fuselage after the putty had set.

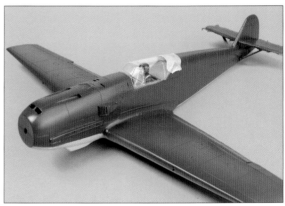

This early Emil was painted with Gunze acrylics applied with the Testor Aztek A470 airbrush. Here, the lower colour of RLM 65 and the upper surface base colour, RLM 71 Dark Green, have been applied.

Next, Gunze H65 Black Green was sprayed in a typical early war splinter pattern. The camouflage was painted freehand, but a fairly hard edge was attempted.

The next two colours represented JG 53's camouflage experiment. RLM 02 was applied according to illustrations in several books.

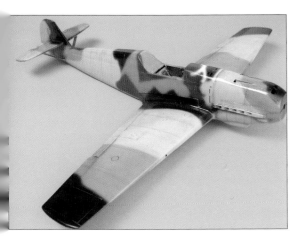

Patches of RLM 65 Light Blue, usually a lower surface shade, was sprayed over the other three colours. Streaks of white were apparently also present forward of the windscreen and underneath the lower surface *Balkenkreuze*.

Decals were scrounged from the spares box, and applied over a coat of Future floor polish. An oil wash has just been brushed on, hence the spotty and dirty appearance.

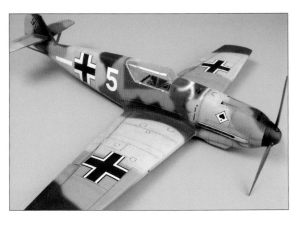

A final coat of Gunze Flat Clear tones down the weathering.

To complement the in-flight display, the kit propeller blades were replaced with photo-etched 'Prop Blur' blades. This required careful preparation of the kit parts.

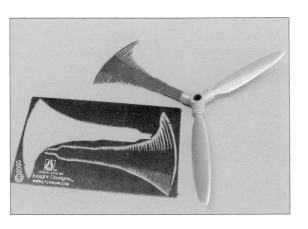

Prop Blur conveys an interesting effect for in-flight displays.

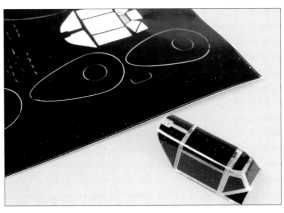

Black Magic self-adhesive vinyl masks were applied to the kit canopy.

accomplish this flat, shallow slope. Fortunately, Hobbycraft's plastic was quite soft and easy to work with. The rough sanded finish was smoothed with progressively finer grit sandpaper, starting with 400 grit, then 100, and moving on to Micro-Mesh cloths to obtain an even surface ready for paint.

One more task remained before I armed myself with the airbrush. A hole was drilled in the bottom of the fuselage into which a length of plastic tube was glued. The tube was to act as a guide for the brass rod on which the model was to be mounted. Gaps around the plastic tube were filled with Milliput. When this epoxy putty had thoroughly set, the overhanging length of tube was sliced off flush with the bottom of the fuselage.

Painting

In the first months of the war, Luftwaffe fighter camouflage comprised a combination of RLM 71 Dark Green and RLM 70 Black Green on the sides and upper surfaces. This dark, low contrast scheme was appropriate for the deep forests of Eastern Europe and for concealment under trees and in shadows, but was unsuitable for aggressive operations in the West. JG 53 experimented with

A length of brass rod was inserted in the plastic tube, connecting the model to its base.

some alternative schemes between the end of the Polish campaign and the start of the invasion of France and the Low Countries. I decided to try out one of these experimental schemes.

First, the model was painted in the standard day-fighter camouflage of the day. The splinter pattern of RLM 70 and 71 was sprayed freehand, but with a fairly hard-edged pattern.

The two disruptive colours of RLM 02 Grey and RLM 65 Light Blue were sprayed with a softer edged demarcation, suggesting its field application. Weathering commenced with an overall wash of thinned raw umber oil paint. With the wash dry, a heavy coat of Future floor polish was sprayed overall to provide a glossy base for the decals.

The simple markings were sourced from the decal spares box, and sealed with a final coat of Gunze Gloss Clear.

Black Magic self-adhesive vinyl masks eliminated a lot of the pain normally associated with painting canopy frames, but the canopy itself was undersized. A noticeable step ran all the way along the sides and the top of the canopy.

As the model was to be depicted in flight, I used a product called 'Prop Blur' to represent a spinning propeller. These photo-etched blades deliver an interesting effect to the display. The kit blades were cut off the propeller hub, and each pitch collar was carefully slotted with a razor saw to accommodate the new photo-etched part.

Conclusion

Hobbycraft's Bf 109E kits will be good practice for new or younger modellers. They are inexpensive and fit together easily – nothing to intimidate the less-experienced recruit. However, unless price is your main consideration, Hobbycraft's kits have otherwise been totally surpassed by both Hasegawa and Tamiya.

In retrospect, there are a few errors that I was either too late or too lazy to correct. First, I did not relocate the position of the machine-gun holes in the wing leading edge. The holes for the machine guns should actually be further inboard. I also should have replaced the undersized canopy with a vacuum-formed replacement. I cut out a Falcon E-1/3 canopy, and it fitted perfectly. During early construction I should have blanked off the wing radiators too.

It is far from perfect, but at least now I have a Messerschmitt Bf 109E-1 wearing an interesting camouflage scheme without too much effort.

In this image, the model has simply been photographed against a model railway scenic background. The mounting rod has been deleted and the brass 'Prop Blur' been blurred a little more in Photoshop. Easy, but not terribly convincing.

ABOVE In this sequence of in-flight shots, the model and the sky were photographed separately then brought together thanks to the magic of Photoshop, and a couple of hours of mucking around.

BELOW The Prop Blur was temporarily replaced with the propeller assembly from Hasegawa's Bf 109E-3 kit. A hair dryer was used to spin the propeller while the photo was being taken.

A silk purse from 1970s plastic?

Subject:	*Messerschmitt Bf 109E-3*
Modeller:	*Brett Green*
Skill level:	*Advanced*
Base kit:	*Matchbox Bf 109 'Emil'*
Scale:	*1/32*
Additional detailing sets used:	*Cutting Edge cockpit; Cutting Edge wheel wells; True Details resin wheels; MDC 1/32-scale riveting tool; plastic strip, wire and scrap pieces*
Paints:	*Gunze acrylics using a Testor Aztek A470 airbrush*
Markings:	*EagleCals EC 50 Major Hans 'Assi' Hahn Part 1*

Matchbox 1/32-scale Messerschmitt Bf 109 Emil in the box

1977 was the year that I finished high school, bought my first car, started a full time job and met the girl who would eventually become my wife. *Looking for Mr Goodbar*, *The Spy Who Loved Me* and *Saturday Night Fever* were showing at the movies, and our transistor radios blared hits from The Eagles, ELO, Donna Summer and The Bee Gees.

1977 was also the year that Matchbox released their 1/32-scale Messerschmitt Bf 109 'Emil'.

The big Bf 109 was a typical Matchbox offering from this era. It was moulded in three colours, boasting 'no painting required for younger modellers'. In common with its Matchbox stablemates, the famous 'Mad Trencher' was apparently at work here as evidenced by deep, wide panel lines.

Looking past these eccentricities, the kit really was quite respectable. Overall shape was accurate – much better than the contemporary 1/32-scale Hasegawa Bf 109E. The Matchbox kit included a nice cockpit, full engine bay and wing machine guns, although some detail was a bit simplified and soft. Parts breakdown was sensible, making for an easy build, and fit was very good.

The main shortcomings were a featureless face to the supercharger intake, solid shroud for the exhausts and a too-conical spinner. Surprisingly, although the kit featured separate ailerons, elevators and rudder, there was no option to display dropped slats or flaps. The thick clear parts were accurately shaped, but the canopy centre section was almost unusable thanks to heavy attachment tabs running along the bottom of each side.

Building a better beast

The basic shapes in the kit cockpit are creditable, but the level of detail is nowhere near 21st-century standards, especially in a model this big. Cutting Edge Modelworks produces a resin replacement cockpit for Hasegawa's 1/32-scale Bf 109. Test fitting showed that the resin cockpit floor would need major surgery to fit in the Matchbox kit. The sidewalls, on the other hand, simply needed to be shortened at the front and back. A hybrid solution was found. The Matchbox kit floor and rear bulkhead would be combined with the resin sidewalls, control column, rudder pedals, seat and instrument panel.

The Cutting Edge sidewalls were shortened and glued to the inside of the kit fuselage. The plastic kit floor and bulkhead were detailed with styrene strip,

Matchbox 1/32-scale Messerschmitt Bf 109 'Emil'

Pros
- Accurate outlines
- Reasonable level of detail
- Good fit
- Recessed panel lines
- Separate ailerons, elevators and rudder

Cons
- Wide, soft panel lines and heavy fabric detail
- Some soft and oversimplified detail
- Thick, clear parts
- Some tricky sink marks
- Poorly shaped spinner and exhaust shrouds
- No option for dropped slats or flaps
- May be difficult to source

ABOVE Hans 'Assi' Hahn's Messerschmitt Bf 109E-3 while 3./JG 2 was still based in Germany during the late spring of 1940. Note that this Bf 109E-3 has been retrofitted with the squared-off canopy normally associated with the E-4 variant.

BELOW These multi-coloured sprues offer a clue to the 1970s origins of the 1/32-scale Matchbox Messerschmitt Bf 109E kit. Despite the coloured plastic, paint will most definitely be required!

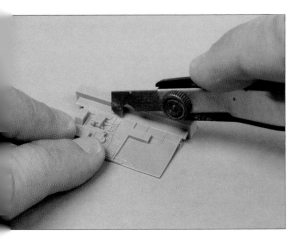

Detail is not up to 21st-century standards, so Cutting Edge's resin cockpit was used to improve the kit. A range of tools, including this scriber, was used to remove the resin parts from their blocks.

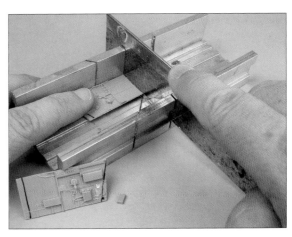

The engineering and shape of the Matchbox cockpit is quite different from the Hasegawa kit, for which these resin parts have been designed. The Cutting Edge sidewalls were modified to fit the Matchbox kit.

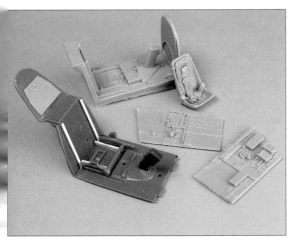

Rather than apply major surgery to the resin cockpit floor and bulkheads, the kit part was adapted.

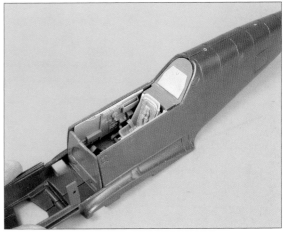

Test fitting is always important, especially with a kitbashing project such as this. Here, the major cockpit components are tested for fit before the parts are committed to glue.

treadplate and fuse wire before all the cockpit components were test fitted. The large trim wheel had to be relocated forward to maintain its original relationship with the back of the sidewall. Gluing styrene strip to the top of the seat mount boosted the height of the resin seat.

The completed cockpit subassemblies were given a base covering of Tamiya XF-1 Flat Black paint, followed by Gunze H70 RLM 02 sprayed in several light coats at a slightly downward angle. This technique preserves a trace of black paint in natural shadow areas. Flat white was mixed with RLM 02 Grey, which was then sprayed in fine streaks and a few random mottles on the sidewalls, seat and rear bulkhead. The final weathering step was a selective wash of thinned raw umber. The oil paint was applied along the edge of boxes and structural detail using a fine brush. When applied subtly, this oil wash represents grime quite well. The cockpit detail of switches, handles, seat cushion, harness straps, buckles, instrument bezels, electrical wiring, hoses and the oxygen regulator were all picked out with acrylic paint and a fine brush.

Resin sidewalls were glued to the fuselage sides. The ammunition bins and machine guns are kit parts. They are quite accurate but detail is a little lacking and the moulding is soft.

The Cutting Edge cockpit subassemblies after careful painting and weathering. This cockpit represents a major improvement over the primitive kit parts.

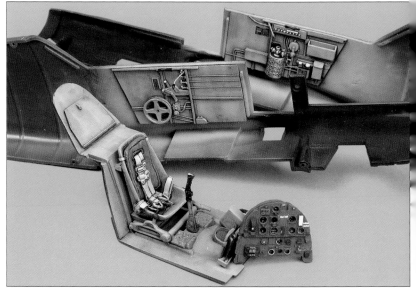

Reheat stencil decals were applied to a number of structures on the cockpit sidewalls. These decals look very effective in this large scale.

I next prepared the wings for Cutting Edge's 1/32-scale resin wheel well set. The Matchbox wheel wells are semi-enclosed, so the short raised ridges around the openings on the lower wings were ground down with a motor tool.

Before securing the wheel wells, the moulded-on slats and flaps were cut from the wings. This was done very carefully, as I wanted to re-attach the excised flaps and slats in the dropped position. I started by deepening panel lines with a scriber, and then completed the job with a new hobby knife.

With the wings prepared, the nicely detailed wheel wells were secured to the lower wings with superglue. A small gap at the front of each wheel well was filled with Gunze Mr Surfacer. The tops of the resin wheel wells were trimmed and sanded slightly to ensure a good fit between the upper and lower wing sections.

Removing the slats left a gaping cavity in the front of the wings. This was blanked off with styrene strip. Four tiny tabs of scrap plastic were glued

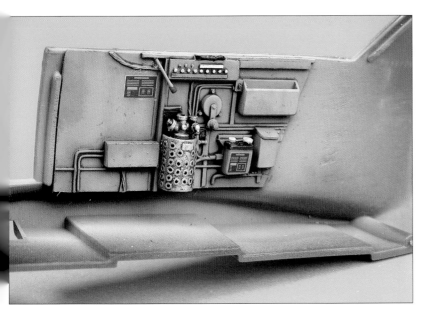

Reheat placard stencil decals are especially effective in this large scale. The silver housing for the oxygen bottle is also very prominent in the Bf 109E cockpit.

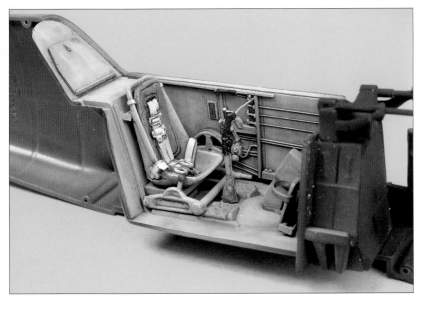

The pale RLM 02 colour used in early Bf 109 cockpit permits the modeller to show off interior detail to good effect. The seat includes a cushion and full harness, both cast in place and simply requiring a careful paint job.

under the upper lip of each opening to support the blanking strip. The top and bottom sections of the slats, previously cut from the wing, were glued together.

At the rear of the wing, the flaps also needed some work before they could be re-attached. Contrail plastic tube was glued to the top front lip of each flap. The gap between the rod and the kit flap was filled with Milliput and sanded smooth when dry.

I knew that I wanted to do something to de-emphasize the wide recessed panel lines, but I was still not sure exactly what to do. Options included heavy sanding of the entire kit surface, or filling and rescribing the panel lines. Instead, I decided on a strategy of distraction. I would apply rivets to the entire airframe, drawing the eye away from the big panel lines – in theory!

A number of modellers' riveting tools have appeared on the market recently. One of the nicest is from MDC of England. It comprises a wooden handle, a steel punch with a circular tip and two photo-etched guides.

Cutting Edge also offers a resin wheel well set. This has also been designed for the Hasegawa kit, so some modifications are in order.

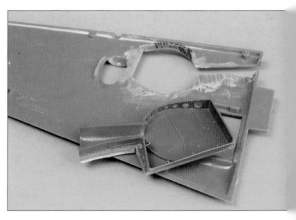

The raised lip of the semi-enclosed wheel well is ground off each bottom wing using a cutting wheel fitted in a Dremel motor tool.

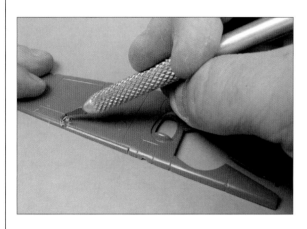

There are no aftermarket slats or flaps available for the Matchbox Bf 109, so we are on our own. All flying surfaces are therefore cut from the wing by first deepening the panel lines with a scriber, then completing separation with a sharp hobby knife.

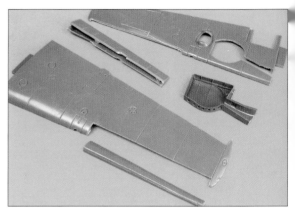

Great care should be employed, as we will be re-fitting the excised flaps and slats in dropped positions.

Armed with the tool and a Bf 109E rivet diagram from a Japanese publication, I set to work. Alignment marks were drawn onto the kit parts using a lead pencil, and the guide was temporarily held between the alignment marks using sticky tape. The rivet punch was then moved painstakingly from guide groove to guide groove until a single line of rivets were completed. Completely measuring, markings and riveting each fuselage side and wing half took between two and three hours. After my fourth riveting session I decided I could live without fully riveted lower wings!

Although the process is tedious, the results are worth the time and effort. To my eye, the rivets are not too prominent, but they certainly dilute the effect of the heavy panel lines.

The speed of subsequent construction was a pleasing contrast to the monotony of riveting. Even though I was not planning to display the engine, it is nevertheless a structural part of the model, mounting the machine guns and the propeller assembly. Also, glimpses of engine detail may be seen through the open cowl vents, so the work is not completely wasted. As a concession to the thick resin instrument panel, I cut off the breeches of the cowl machine guns and the back half of the platform mounting the guns.

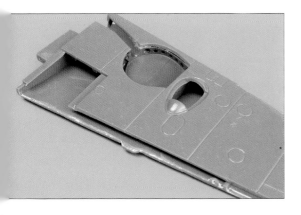

The wheel wells fit with a little more fiddling and a lot of superglue. A narrow gap at the front of the wheel well will be dealt with later using Gunze Mr Surfacer 1000.

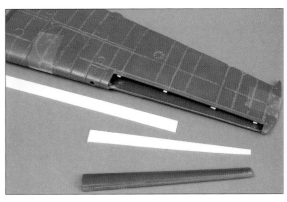

Tiny plastic tabs are fitted to the upper lip of the slat cavity. These support the styrene sheet that will blank off the open space behind the slats.

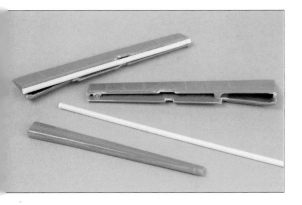

Contrail plastic tube was used to re-profile the top leading edge of the flaps. The top and bottom halves of each slat, cut earlier from the wing halves, were glued together.

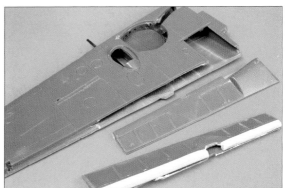

The gap between the Contrail rod and the top of the flap was filled with Milliput, a white two-part epoxy putty.

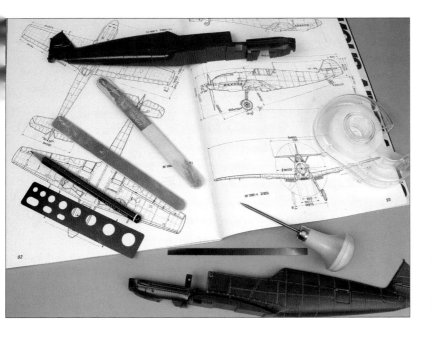

The entire fuselage and the upper wings received lines of rivets using MDC's 1/32-scale rivet-making tool. This is a punch with a tiny circle at its tip. A photo-etched metal guide ensures accurate spacing for each rivet.

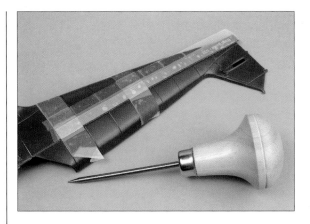

First, the guide is taped to the kit part.

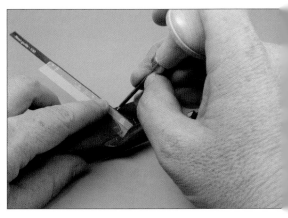

The guide is then rested gently in the first slot in the guide, and pressed firmly home, leaving a perfectly circular rivet mark – hopefully!

Repeat this process many thousands of times and you have a model that somewhat resembles a heavily used pincushion! A coat of paint will mute this exaggerated appearance.

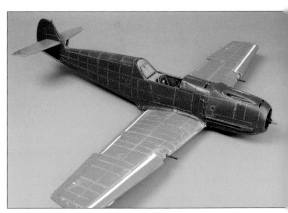

The overall fit of this old model is very good, even after modifications to squeeze in a new cockpit and wheel well, and the stress of surface riveting.

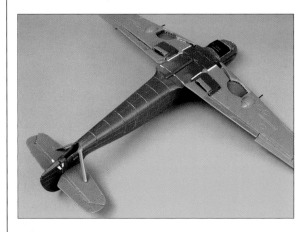

A few gaps at the lower wing root were covered by thin strips of plastic card.

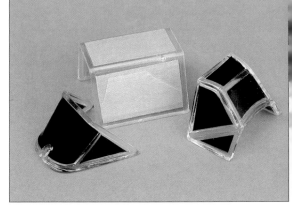

Black Magic masks take the tedium away from the task of canopy masking. The thick, unsightly centre canopy section from the Matchbox kit was replaced with its Hasegawa counterpart. The clear Hasegawa plastic was masked with Tamiya tape.

The model received a base coat of Gunze H70 RLM 02. Camouflage masks were improvised from scrap cardboard, stood off the surface of the model by small blobs of Blu-Tack.

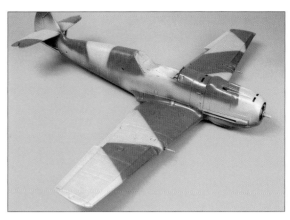

The result is a camouflage demarcation that has a feathered, but fairly hard, edge. Gunze H64 RLM 71 Dark Green was used for the second camouflage colour.

The top colours were masked and Gunze H67 RLM 65 Light Blue was sprayed on the undersurfaces and up the fuselage sides. The same feathered demarcation was employed for this colour.

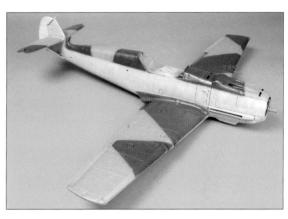

Streaks and spots of a paler shade were sprayed onto all three camouflage colours to obtain a subtle weathering effect.

An oil wash of thinned raw umber paint was brushed over the entire model to further bring out details. The effect looks extreme here, as the wash is still wet.

The model received an overall coat of Tamiya Clear before decals were applied. Markings were sourced from Eagle Cals EC50, 'Major Hans "Assi" Hahn Special Airbrushed Edition Part 1'.

The fit of the fuselage halves was flawless. They virtually clicked together. One nice touch is the bevelled edges of the fuselage spine. When the fuselage halves are glued together, a convincing panel line runs along the top centre line. The wings fitted well at the upper wing root but needed some attention on the bottom halves. The tail, control surfaces and stabilizer struts were added without incident or the requirement for filler.

Matchbox did not include the rudder actuators in their kit, so I built them from scratch. Plastic rod was used for the fairings, brass rod for the control wires and small pieces of plastic for the horizontal posts on the rudder. The actuators were attached to the empennage just above the bottom mount of the strut.

The subject aircraft was a Bf 109E-3 but it had been retrofitted with the E-4 canopy, which was quite a common occurrence. The thick canopy centre section was replaced with its counterpart from Hasegawa's Bf 109E-4. Hasegawa's part is much thinner and clearer. The only disadvantage is a raised locating line on the inside top of the canopy for the head armour, which was not fitted to this aircraft. Before painting, two small discs of plastic were glued to the inside of the canopy, representing the knobs on the front of the sliding windows.

Painting

Although I usually start by painting the lower surface colour, this time I painted the top camouflage first. On this style of camouflage from mid-1940, it looks as though the RLM 65 Light Blue colour has been sprayed over existing paint on the fuselage to create a new, high demarcation line. I decided to follow the same sequence.

The model received an overall base coat of RLM 02 Grey. The disruptive colour of RLM 71 Dark Green was sprayed with the aid of cardboard masks, fractionally held off the surface of the model with small blobs of Blu-Tack. This resulted in a slightly feathered demarcation between the colours. RLM 65 Light Blue was then applied to the undersurfaces and up the fuselage side. The same masking technique was used to achieve a soft demarcation between the upper and lower colours.

Several thin coats of Gunze H20 Flat Clear toned and blend the various weathering measures. Smaller subassemblies including the propeller, undercarriage and canopy, have been glued in place to complete the model.

ABOVE To my eye, the rivet detail draws attention away from the kit's heavy panel lines. The dropped slats and flaps add interest to the large expanse of those 1/32-scale wings too.

BELOW Antenna wire has been added from nylon monofilament. Isolators are tiny blobs of superglue, built up with larger blobs of Krystal Kleer. Note the scratch-built rudder actuators above the tail wheel.

Paler shades of each colour were mixed and sprayed in fine lines and random mottles as an initial weathering measure. An oil wash of heavily thinned raw umber paint further emphasized panel lines and other structural details.

When the oil wash had dried, the model was sprayed with an overall coat of Tamiya Clear. This gloss coat prepared the plastic for the markings from EagleCals' 1/32-scale decal sheet, 'Major Hans "Assi" Hahn Special Airbrushed Edition Part 1'. For some unknown reason the fuselage crosses refused to settle into the deep panel lines. I removed the partially cured decals and replaced them with *Balkenkreuze* from another EagleCals set. These decals performed without problems. Fortunately, the unique markings did not suffer the same fate as the national markings. The big White 13 and III Gruppe bar conformed closely to the panel lines and rivets with a few brushed applications of Micro Set and Micro Sol.

Landing gear legs were detailed with hydraulic lines from fuse wire. The restraining straps for the lines were cut from thin strips of Tamiya masking tape. True Details 1/32-scale resin Bf 109B to G-2 wheels were an improvement over the softly detailed kit parts.

Several thin coats of Gunze acrylic Flat Clear blended the various weathering measures. At this time, the small subassemblies including wheels, undercarriage, canopy and propeller were glued in place.

The project was completed with the installation of slats, pitot tube, aileron mass balances, painting of wing tip navigation lights and the addition of aerial wire. Isolators for the aerial wire were formed from tiny spots of superglue, built up when dry with blobs of Krystal Kleer – a white adhesive similar to wood glue. When the isolators were dry, they were painted light grey. The rear third of each isolator was then painted black. This lends the impression of a white cone when viewed from certain angles.

Matchbox's 1/32-scale Bf 109E is an underrated kit which can look great with a little extra effort.

Looking at my completed model, however, there are a few other issues that I would address next time. The conical and oversimplified propeller spinner really lets down the nose. The easiest solution would be to replace this with the Hasegawa spinner. I would also add vertical grille detail to the supercharger intake face. Finally, a solid shroud hems in the exhaust stacks on the kit. This should really be thinner at the top and the bottom, completely open at the rear and have a ventilation hole at the front.

The propeller spinner and supercharger intakes remain weak points, but the model otherwise fares well considering it is a relic of the 1970s!

Reich defence Emil

Subject:	Messerschmitt Bf 109E-3
Construction:	Brett Green
Painting and markings:	Chris Wauchop
Skill level:	Advanced
Base kit:	Tamiya Bf 109E-4; ICM Bf 109E-3
Scale:	1/72
Additional detailing sets used:	Aires Bf 109E cockpit set (for Tamiya); plastic strip, wire and scrap pieces
Paints:	Gunze acrylics using a Testor Aztek A470 airbrush
Markings:	Cutting Edge 48190 (bonus 1/72-scale markings)

Tamiya's and ICM's Messerschmitt Bf 109E-3 and E-4 kits in the box

Tamiya's 1/72-scale Bf 109E-3 and E-4 kits were released in the year 2000. Each contains 47 parts in medium grey plastic and three parts in clear. These models are typical of Tamiya's high-quality offerings, with flawless moulding, crisp panel lines, good detail, perfect fit and simple construction breakdown.

The single grey sprue is identical in both kits. Useful options include all three styles of propeller spinner, drop tank, bomb and tropical filter. Tamiya supplies one style of canopy with each model. The transparent plastic is thin and crystal clear but the windscreen and centre section are joined, so the modeller will have to break out the razor saw to display the canopy open.

The only real shortcoming of this excellent kit is that the fuselage is approximately 2.5mm short when compared to respected plans.

ICM's Bf 109E family appeared a few years later. These kits are moulded in soft white plastic. They do not include drop tanks, bombs or racks, but at first glance the parts appear otherwise identical to Tamiya's. Closer inspection reveals some nasty sink marks in the turbocharger intake and the top of the flaps that will be tricky to repair. Some of the detail is softer too, notably the wheels and some cockpit parts. Both kits include canopies for the Bf 109E-3 and E-4. These canopies are supplied in three pieces each, making it a simple matter to display the cockpit, but the clear plastic is thick and slightly distorted compared to Tamiya's parts.

The biggest difference, however, is the fuselage. It is the correct length.

Combining the Tamiya and ICM kits for an accurate Emil

So, we have a perfectly moulded Emil with a short fuselage, and a different brand of kit with almost identical parts breakdown and the correct length fuselage but some moulding flaws.

2.5mm might not sound like a big difference, but the Tamiya rear fuselage is perceptively shorter when compared to its ICM counterpart. ICM's kit actually costs less than many 1/72-scale accessory sets, so it was a logical decision to combine the best aspects of each model.

Test fitting proved that Tamiya's and ICM's parts were interchangeable, making for a straightforward kitbashing project.

Before the main parts were assembled, I prepared Aires' 1/72-scale Bf 109E cockpit. This is a nicely detailed set, with the main elements in resin and

Tamiya 1/72-scale Messerschmitt Bf 109E-3 and E-4 kits
Pros
- Crisp surface detail
- Flawless moulding
- Good level of detail
- Excellent fit
- Thin and crystal clear transparencies
- Useful options
- Generally accurate

Cons
- Fuselage is 2.5mm too short
- Two-piece canopy still needs to be cut in order to be displayed open
- No option for dropped slats or flaps

ICM 1/72-scale Messerschmitt Bf 109E-3 and E-4 kits
Pros
- Crisp surface detail
- Good level of detail
- Fair fit
- Accurate
- Includes both E-3 and E-4 canopies
- Useful options
- Inexpensive

Cons
- Some big sink marks in hard-to-eliminate places
- Soft plastic prone to warpage
- No option for dropped slats or flaps
- Somewhat distorted clear parts

The Messerschmitt Bf 109E soldiered on well after the Battle of Britain. This Bf 109E-3 undertook Reich Defence duties with JG 1 in late 1942.

photo-etched details including harness, instrument panel and tiny handles. Raised details moulded to ICM's fuselage sidewalls were ground flat with a motor tool, and the resin parts were painted. According to my usual method, I applied a dark wash of thinned oil paint to the grey cockpit parts. Disaster! The oil wash dried unevenly and actually stripped off the acrylic paint in places. I assume that I must have accidentally thinned the oil paint with alcohol instead of turpentine.

The oil wash was scrubbed off and cockpit parts were re-sprayed as required. Details including the harness straps, buckles, oxygen regulator, switches and handles were picked out with acrylic paint using a very fine brush.

Cockpit parts were installed and the ICM fuselage halves were assembled. This was somewhat easier said than done. ICM's white plastic is quite soft. Surface detail is as crisp as Tamiya's, but the fuselage halves were warped. To correct this warpage, the tail was first glued and clamped. When this section had set, liquid glue was run into the joins on the spine and along the bottom of the fuselage. Alignment was established by tape until the glue dried. Finally, the nose was secured at the top and the sides using plastic clamps before liquid glue was brushed along the remaining join lines. The separate top and bottom cowl also required extra work to guarantee perfect alignment. Fortunately, the soft plastic made this manipulation fairly painless.

By contrast with the fuselage, Tamiya's wings were assembled in minutes.

ICM's fuselage proved to be an almost perfect match for Tamiya's wings, tailplanes and supercharger intake. The only area that needed more attention was the bottom wing-to-fuselage join. A little trimming of ICM's fuselage and a few swipes with the sanding stick after assembly ensured a good fit.

Although ICM's clear parts permit the canopy to be displayed open, the quality of Tamiya's transparencies is undoubtedly superior. The fit of Tamiya's canopy is also better, even on ICM's fuselage. Tamiya's canopy was therefore prepared for paint with Eduard's 1/72-scale self-adhesive masks, saving a lot of time from an otherwise fiddly job.

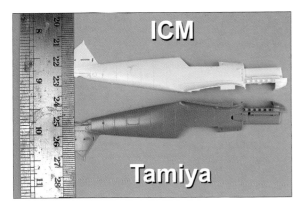

Compared to respected plans, Tamiya's 1/72-scale fuselage is around 2.5mm too short. ICM's fuselage length appears to conform to plans.

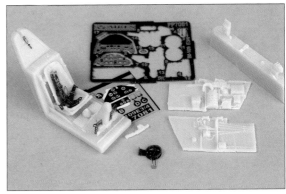

Aires produces a well-detailed multimedia cockpit for Tamiya's 1/72-scale Messerschmitt Bf 109E kits. This cockpit is also suitable for ICM's Emils.

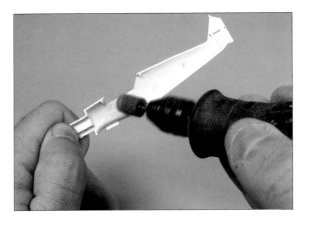

Raised detail moulded to the fuselage sidewalls is removed using a grinding attachment in the Dremel motor tool. A light touch is required to avoid damaging the surrounding plastic.

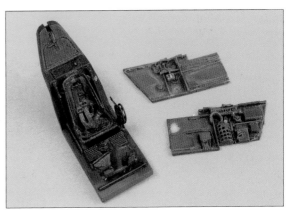

Sometimes, weathering goes wrong. The oil wash dried unevenly in places, did not dry at all in others, and damaged the base acrylic paint.

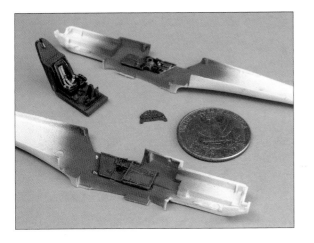

The oil wash was scrubbed off and the cockpit parts were selectively resprayed. Details including the harness, buckles, oxygen regulator, switches and handles, were picked out with a fine brush.

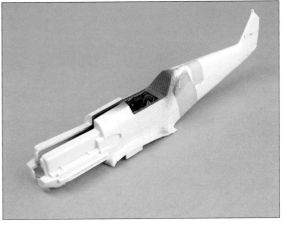

Detail on the ICM fuselage halves is crisp, but the soft plastic is prone to warpage. The fuselage halves were joined in stages, starting with the tail and moving forward.

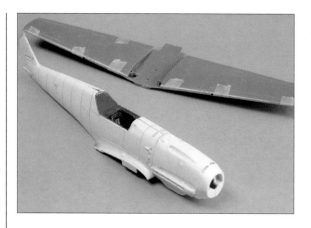

The top and bottom engine cowl also required manipulation before securing with liquid glue. The extra effort was rewarded with an almost perfect fit. Tamiya's wings were assembled in minutes with no problems whatsoever.

No painting required? Tamiya's grey wings, horizontal tailplanes, rudder and supercharger intake mated perfectly with ICM's fuselage.

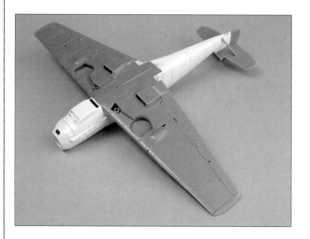

A little tweaking was required where the trailing centre section of the wing meets the bottom of the fuselage. A few swipes with a sanding stick ensured a gap-free fit in this area too.

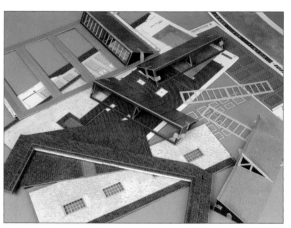

This HO scale bus station will double as a Luftwaffe hangar for the model. The building is die-cut cardboard, and is quite simple to build.

Painting

A number of Bf 109Es soldiered on beyond the Battle of Britain and Channel dogfighting to serve in Germany and on the Eastern Front. One such aircraft that caught my eye was Yellow 8 of 12./JG 1, which performed Reich Defence duties in spring 1942. This was a Bf 109E-3 that had been retrofitted with the later-style Bf 109E-4 canopy. Several photos of this aircraft appear on page 66 of Eric Mombeek's book, *Defenders of the Reich – Jagdgeschwader 1 Volume 1 1939–1942*.

The lower surfaces and fuselage sides of the model received a base coat of Gunze H67 RLM 65 Light Blue. The upper surface camouflage pattern of Gunze H70 RLM 02 Grey and Gunze H64 RLM 71 Dark Green was sprayed freehand using the new metal-bodied Aztek airbrush fitted with the fine Tan tip. A heavy mottle was applied to the fuselage sides using photos in Eric Mombeek's book as a guide.

The propeller spinner and blades were painted Gunze H65 RLM 70 Black Green with the prominent pitch collars finished in Tamiya XF-16 Flat

When completed, the building can be combined with a base and background to replicate a wartime airfield.

The model was painted with Gunze acrylics using the Testor Aztek A470 airbrush.

Aluminium. When dry, the pitch collars received a dark oil wash to highlight details.

Weathering commenced with a thin mix of Tamiya XF-1 Flat Black and XF-64 Red Brown sprayed along panel lines and other structural features. The same mix was used to add heavier streaking behind the exhaust and above the wing root panel. Panel lines were further highlighted by running a thin wash of Tamiya X-18 Semi-Gloss Black mixed with water. A silver pencil was used to simulate chipping of the paint on the wing root area – a typical sign of wear and tear on Bf 109s.

Undercarriage legs were painted Gunze acrylic H70 RLM 02 before also being treated to a squirt of the dirty Black Brown mix.

Tyres were painted of Gunze H77 Tyre Black, with the edges lightened using Tamiya XF-52 Flat Earth.

The semi-gloss Gunze paint was buffed to a high shine in preparation for decals.

Markings were sourced from Cutting Edge's 1/48-scale sheet 48190 'Bf 109 Emils Part 3'. This sheet includes bonus decals for four aircraft in 1/72 scale, including Yellow 8 of JG 1. The decal instructions point out that the JG 1 badges were probably not worn on both sides of the fuselage, but it seemed a shame to leave these extra markings on the decal sheet!

Several thin coats of Gunze Flat Clear blended the decals and paintwork behind a uniformly matt finish.

ABOVE Decals were sourced from Cutting Edge's sheet number 4848190. Bonus 1/72-scale markings are supplied.

BELOW Panel lines were highlighted with careful application of a thinned dark brown mix.

ABOVE ICM's fuselage is longer than that provided by Tamiya, providing a correctly proportioned Emil.

BELOW The Tamiya kit includes many useful options; including three different styles of propeller spinner, drop tank and bomb.

Yellow-nose raider

Subject:	*Messerschmitt Bf 109E-4*
Construction:	*Brett Green*
Painting and markings:	*Chris Wauchop*
Skill level:	*Advanced*
Base Kit:	*Hasegawa Bf 109E-4*
Scale:	*1/48*
Additional detailing sets used:	*Teknics Bf 109E Exterior Upgrade Set; Cutting Edge Cockpit; various plastic and metal strip, sheet and scrap*
Paints:	*Gunze and Tamiya Acrylics applied with the Testor Aztek metal-bodied airbrush.*
Markings:	*EagleCals EC50 Major Hans 'Assi' Hahn Part 1.*

Hasegawa's 1/48-scale Messerschmitt Bf 109E kits in the box

The late 1980s saw a resurgence in 1/48-scale plastic model kit releases. Not only did the quantity increase, the quality did too.

One of the early examples of a new-generation World War II model kit was Hasegawa's Bf 109E. This was released in 1988, and featured crisply engraved panel lines, separate slats and flaps, photo-etched detailing parts, plenty of useful options including drop tanks and bombs, plus crystal clear canopy parts.

The first four kits, however, suffered from an inaccurately shaped nose and an overly long fuselage. The errors are quite obvious when the kit fuselage is compared to respected plans. These original, inaccurate kits were labeled J1, J2, J3 and J4.

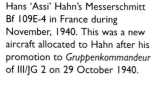

Hans 'Assi' Hahn's Messerschmitt Bf 109E-4 in France during November, 1940. This was a new aircraft allocated to Hahn after his promotion to *Gruppenkommandeur* of III/JG 2 on 29 October 1940.

To their credit, Hasegawa recognized the problem and released a newly tooled family of Bf 109Es in 1993. These new kits maintained the high points of Hasegawa's original Emils, but featured an all-new fuselage, engine cowling and several other corrected detail parts. This model eclipsed all other Bf 109E kits available at the time.

The corrected kits may be easily identified by the 'JT' prefix in front of the item number.

Hasegawa has released at least 19 variations of their new Bf 109E kits since 1993. We have seen the Bf 109E-1, E-3, E-4, E-7, Tropical and even the carrier-based Bf 109T. Three common sprues contain 53 parts in grey plastic. Some kits include additional sprues with parts for drop tank, trop filter and alternate spinners. Kit numbers JT11, JT12 and JT123 provide canopies for both the Bf 109E-3 and E-4, but the remaining kits only offer a single version. Kit numbers 09369 and 09482 are boxed as Bf 109E-1 kits. Both supply a resin plug to backfill the lower wing cannon bulges, but it is up to the modeller to grind off the bulge, relocate the gun ports and fill the panel lines on the wings. Kit number 09326 is the Bf 109T with resin wing tips and supercharger intake.

Hasegawa's Bf 109E-4/7/Trop kit was also offered under Revell's label, but photo-etched parts were not included in this release.

A nose job for Emil

Teknics from the USA produced a multimedia airframe upgrade kit for Hasegawa's original, flawed Bf 109E kits. This comprehensive upgrade comprised a new solid nose, replacement control surfaces with beautiful fabric tape detail, 250kg bomb and rack, 300-litre drop tank and rack, wheels, photo-etched wheel well liners, wing radiator flaps and faces, command pennants for the antenna mast, rudder actuators, tie-down hooks, gear doors, canopy framing and perforated faces for the forward fuselage and the spinner backplate.

I had been looking for an excuse to use this upgrade for quite a while. This seemed to be as good a time as any.

Although the new Hasegawa Bf 109E fuselage is accurate, the Teknics nose features better detail. I particularly like the cast-on exhaust stacks, already hollowed out and with a raised 'weld seam' along the centreline. I decided to use as much of the upgrade as possible, including this solid resin nose. As this part was designed for the older kit, I was not sure how it would mate to Hasegawa's retooled fuselage.

A razor saw was used to carefully cut the nose from the Hasegawa fuselage. Test fitting suggested that the resin part would fit well. Initially, I thought that I would not even have to cut off the big casting block behind the resin nose, but some trimming was required to avoid fouling the cockpit elements.

Ailerons and radiator flaps were cut from Hasegawa's wings in preparation for Teknics' resin and photo-etched replacements. The trailing edge of the upper wing halves were bevelled with a sanding stick to ensure a step-free fit for the resin ailerons. The wheel wells presented more of a challenge. The inner wheel well sections had to be removed to make way for photo-etched replacements. The raised curve on the inside of the lower wing was sliced repeatedly with a cutting wheel fitted to my Dremel motor tool. A low speed was selected to avoid melting the surrounding styrene – always a risk when using a motor tool with plastic. The remaining raised ribs were snipped off with a sprue cutter, then cleaned up with a hobby knife and a sanding stick. The inner wheel liner and photo-etched part representing the canvas wheel covers were pressed into place and secured with superglue.

Cutting Edge's 1/48-scale cockpit, item number CEC48379, was selected to add life to the interior. The resin cockpit features deep sidewall detail and a very attractive seat with cushion and harness cast in place. The cockpit parts and the fuselage sidewall were painted and weathered before installation.

Hasegawa 1/48-scale Messerschmitt Bf 109E kits (JT Series)
Pros
- Crisp, appropriate and restrained surface details (panel lines, recessed rivets and subtly raised fabric texture)
- Choice of dropped or raised slats and flaps
- Good fit
- Reasonable level of detail
- Accurate
- Useful options including drop tank, bomb racks and tropical filter
- Photo-etched parts for head armour and radiator/oil cooler grilles.
- Excellent clear parts
Cons
- Decals are sometimes thick, yellowed and can be temperamental in application.
- E-1 variant requires more work from the modeller.

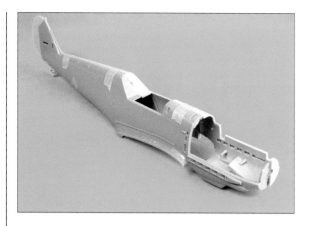

Hasegawa's initial Bf 109E releases suffered from shape and dimensional problems in a number of areas. The light grey fuselage half is Hasegawa's early effort; while the later, more accurate version is in medium grey.

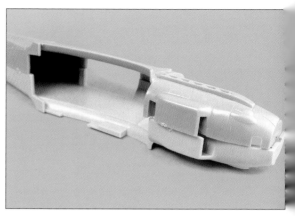

Note the disparity in size, shape and detail between the two fuselage halves. These differences are quite noticeable on finished models.

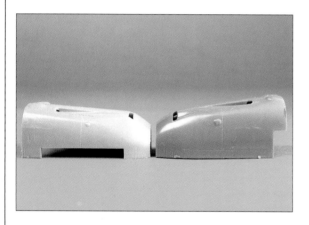

The engine cowl part was also significantly revised on later releases. The discrepancies between height and angle of the upper cowl parts are very clear in this comparison.

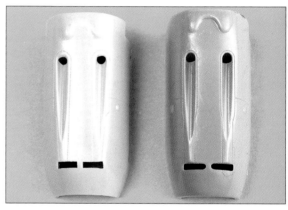

The different shapes and positions of the gun troughs and cooling slots may be clearly seen in this view.

Teknics released an exterior correction set for Hasegawa's original (and flawed) 109E kits. The solid resin nose is the highlight of this set.

Two recently acquired tools are a JLC Razor Saw, and a new style of scriber. Both were sourced from the Czech Republic.

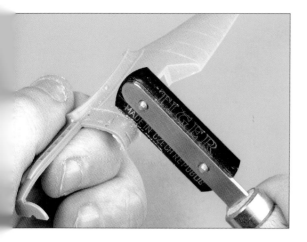

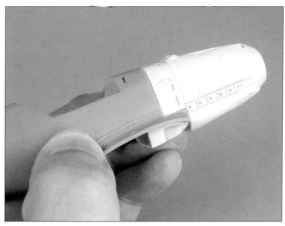

Although it is designed for the early flawed kits, the Teknics nose may be used with Hasegawa's most recent releases. The razor saw made short work of cutting off the forward fuselage.

Teknics' resin nose boasts better detail than even the newer Hasegawa parts. The hollowed-out exhaust stacks, starter dog, cooling slots, latches and panel lines are all very impressive.

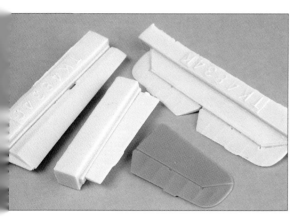

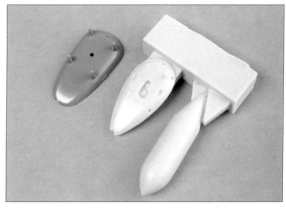

Teknics also supplies replacement control surfaces, which feature very subtle fabric tape detail.

If you are building an E-4/N, E-4/B or E-7/B, the Teknics ETC rack is a much more accurate shape than its kit counterpart.

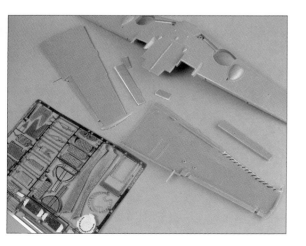

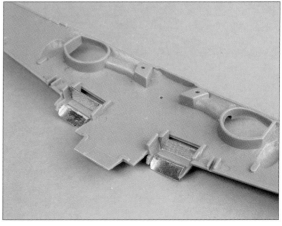

Ailerons and radiator flaps were cut from Hasegawa's kit wings. The trailing edge of the upper wing was thinned with a sanding stick to permit a step-free fit for the resin ailerons.

Teknics' brass radiator faces and flaps add welcome detail to this area.

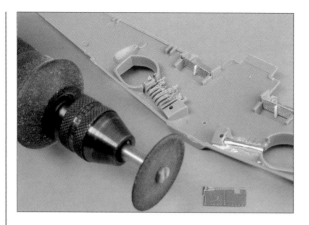

Support braces were added to the front radiator faces using strip styrene. The inner wheel well sections were sliced repeatedly with the Dremel fitted with a cutting wheel in preparation for the installation of photo-etched parts.

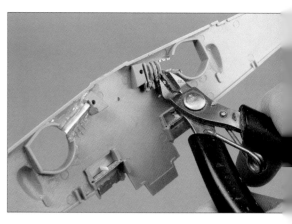

The remaining 'toast rack' was easily removed with a sprue cutter, and then cleaned up with a hobby knife. The brass inner wheel well sections were rolled into shape and installed from the inside of the wing.

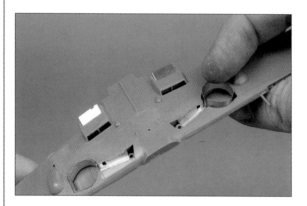

Canvas wheel well covers are also represented in photo-etched brass. These parts were pushed into place, and then pressed into the outer corners to form the correct final shape.

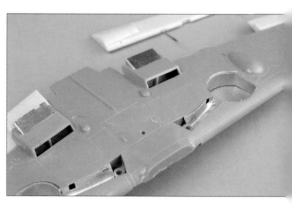

The brass parts certainly lend a noticeable improvement in detail to the lower wings.

Cutting Edge's cockpit, item number CEC48379, was used for this project.

The cockpit parts were tacked to a box using Blu-Tack. These parts were first coated with Tamiya Flat Black, and then sprayed with German Grey before harness and cushion details were picked out with a fine brush.

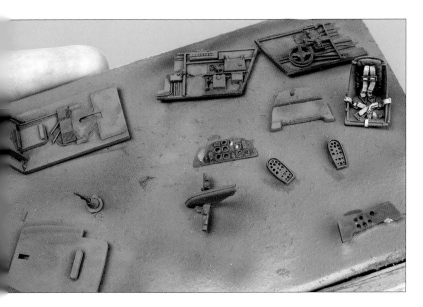

A thin wash of dark oil paint adds further depth to the cockpit parts.

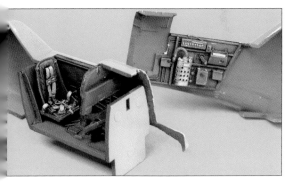

Details such as the oxygen regulator, switches, fuses and handles, were painted before the cockpit was installed. The firewall had to be cut off before the nose could be fitted.

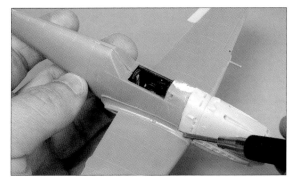

Some additional work was required to obtain a perfect fit for the resin nose, especially around the wing root and lower fuselage join. Mission Models' Micro Chisel is being used here to fair in the wing root.

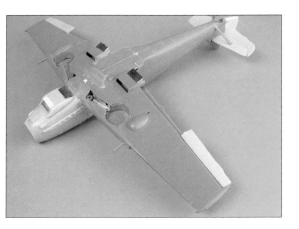

Only minimal filler was required elsewhere on the model.

A few pinholes in the main wheels were filled with two-part epoxy putty. The resin flaps were fitted with steel pins to ensure positive location. The undercarriage legs were detailed with Teknics's gear covers plus hydraulic lines from fine wire.

Tamiya's 1/48-scale Citroen 11CV Traction is a lovely little model, and very simple to build. In this instance the model has been enhanced with a Hauler photo-etched set.

The Hauler set includes many enhancements. The most obvious is the replacement grille, which is a great improvement over the kit part.

A German-style horn and Notek light (on the left mudguard) have been added to this little French car.

A base coat of Tamiya XF-24 German Grey was streaked and mottled to obtain an uneven, weather-beaten appearance.

A thin black oil wash further reinforced the impression of an airfield hack, exposed to the elements for the summer months.

The completed project is a nice little model in its own right, but also makes an ideal airfield accessory.

The moment of truth was approaching. I test fitted the solid resin nose with the fuselage. Although I had trimmed the back of the casting block, it still interfered with the cockpit parts. The firewall and a few millimetres of the cockpit floor were sliced off to accommodate the nose. With this minor surgery complete, the nose was glued to the fuselage with superglue, and the assembled wings were installed. Some additional filling, sanding and trimming was required to fair in the resin nose with the plastic fuselage, especially around the leading edge of the wing root.

The resin control surfaces fitted perfectly. Even the stabilizer struts fell into place without problems. I particularly liked Teknics' added detail for the rudder actuator rods and posts. The leading edge of the landing flaps were drilled and fitted with metal pins to reinforce their join with the wing. Before painting, the landing gear was supplemented with Tecknics' brass gear doors and hydraulic lines from soft copper wire.

Painting and markings

The model was painted in the camouflage colours of Gunze H67 RLM 65 Light Blue, Gunze H70 RLM 02 Grey and Gunze H64 RLM 71 Dark Green. A fairly heavy mottle was applied to the fuselage sides.

The nose, spinner and rudder was finished with a mixture of 60 per cent Tamiya XF-3 Flat Yellow and 40 per cent Gunze H24 Orange Yellow. This bright colour was applied in several thin coats to ensure good coverage. Propeller blades were painted a 50:50 mix of Tamiya XF-27 Black Green and Gunze H65 Black Green.

Wheel hubs received a coat of Tamiya XF-24 Dark Grey, followed by a wash of Flat Black acrylic paint. This helped emphasise the depth of the wheels. Tyres were painted a mix of 40 per cent Tamiya XF-1 Flat Black and 60 per cent

Sharp-eyed readers will note that the aircraft in the background is actually one of 'Assi' Hahn's later mounts. More detail about this one in Volume 2!

Tamiya XF-64 Red Brown. They were then lightly oversprayed with Tamiya XF-53 Flat Earth.

Decals were sourced from EagleCals' 1/48-scale decal sheet, 'Major Hans "Assi" Hahn Special Airbrushed Edition Part 1'

Final details added after painting included a canopy-locking handle from scrap plastic card and stretched sprue, canopy-retaining wire from stretched sprue and the antenna wire from smoke-coloured nylon monofilament (invisible mending thread).

ABOVE It is interesting to note the differences between the camouflage on this aircraft and Hahn's earlier BF 109E-3 from only six months earlier.

BELOW Tamiya's Citroen is an appropriate airfield companion for almost any European Luftwaffe diorama from mid-1940, whether it be in France or on the Eastern Front.

Desert Jabo

Subject:	*Messerschmitt Bf 109E-7/B/Trop*
Modeller:	*Brett Green*
Skill level:	*Advanced*
Base kit:	*Tamiya Bf 109E-4/7 Trop*
Scale:	*1/48*
Additional detailing sets used:	*CMK Bf 109E Engine Set; CMK Bf 109E VDM Propeller Assembly; KMC Bf 109E cockpit; True Details Bf 109B-G-2 wheels; Black Magic canopy masks; plastic strip, wire and scrap pieces*
Paints:	*Polly Scale acrylics using a Testor Aztek A470 airbrush*
Markings:	*Hasegawa decals (from kit No. JT10) and various markings from the spares box*

Tamiya's 1/48-scale Messerschmitt Bf 109E kits in the box

Tamiya released its 1/48-scale Messerschmitt Bf 109E-3 kit in 1996. This was one of the first World War II aircraft kits that Tamiya produced after a long hiatus, and it clearly proclaimed the Japanese company's hallmarks of clever engineering, simple construction and high level of detail.

The shape of the Emil's nose must be particularly tricky to capture in plastic, because the first run of Tamiya's Bf 109E-3 featured a flawed engine cowl. By the time Tamiya released its Bf 109E-4/7 Trop kit in 1998, however, the nose had been re-tooled to an accurate profile. All subsequent production runs of the Bf 109E-3 also included the corrected parts.

Indeed, both kits share identical grey plastic sprues, even though many of the options are not used on the 109E-3 variant. Sixty-six magnificently tooled grey styrene parts are included in the box, with a further five in thin, clear, distortion free plastic.

The kits are engineered with a structurally solid fuselage thanks to a 'blank' engine block moulded into the nose. This reinforces the forward fuselage, ensuring a positive mount to align the upper and lower engine cowls. Separate slats and flaps are supplied, along with a 300-litre drop tank, 250kg bomb, three styles of spinner, trop filter and separate windscreen armour. Surface detail is by way of crisp, fine recessed panel lines and raised fabric-tape detail on control surfaces. Cockpit detail is not bad, but could do with some extra attention or replacement, especially considering that the canopy is designed to be displayed open. Two stout tabs are moulded to the starboard side to secure the canopy in the open position – a very nice touch.

Tamiya's Emil is also a pleasure to build. In fact, this viceless kit would be a perfect beginner's project.

100-hour service

Tamiya's excellent Emil kits have drawn the attention of not only modellers, but also accessory manufacturers. There is a plethora of aftermarket accessories, conversions and detail sets available for these models.

CMK offers a full engine bay, which includes mounts and cowl machine guns. They also supply a well-detailed propeller assembly with a detailed

---

Tamiya 1/48-scale Messerschmitt Bf 109E-3 and E-4 kits

Pros
- Crisp surface detail
- Flawless moulding
- Good level of detail
- Excellent fit
- Thin and crystal clear transparencies
- Separate slats and flaps
- Useful options
- Accurate

Cons
- Cockpit detail a bit lacklustre
- Some adjustment of tailplane struts required

A Messerschmitt Bf 109E-7/B/Trop Jabo of 8./ZG 1 undergoing routine maintenance in North Africa during 1942.

spinner backplate. I thought it would be interesting to combine these with the Tamiya kit for a maintenance scene.

CMK's DB 601 engine is beautifully detailed, but comprises relatively few parts as much of the detail is cast in place. Assembly is nevertheless tricky due to the fragile and tiny parts. The instructions are also vague regarding exact placement of various pipes, wiring and even larger items such as the oil cooler. Additional reference is essential.

I further complicated construction when I dropped the assembled and painted engine on a hard floor, sending engine mounts and machine guns scattering into the darkest and dustiest corners of the room. After too long on my hands and knees I eventually recovered all the parts and assembled the engine for a second time.

Tamiya's kit fuselage was prepared for the engine. The nose was carefully cut off using a razor saw. I was a little too enthusiastic below the gun cowl on the

Tamiya's 1/48-scale Messerschmitt Bf 109 kits are simple to build and quite accurate. There is also a large selection of accessories for this kit.

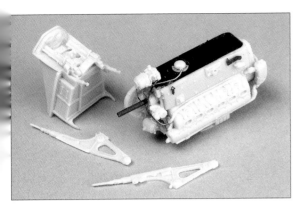

CMK's 1/48-scale Bf 109E engine bay has been specifically designed for Tamiya's Bf 109E-3 and E-4/7 kits. This set contains relatively few parts thanks to clever design, but some experience is required before tackling such a project.

The instructions are a little vague, meaning that additional reference is essential for the correct placement of various pipes, wiring and even larger features such as the oil cooler.

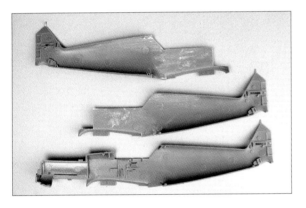

KMC's 1/48-scale resin cockpit was used for this project. The moulded-on sidewall detail was ground off using a motor tool. The forward fuselage was also carefully cut off at this stage. Note the unmodified fuselage half at the bottom of the photo.

KMC's resin cockpit parts, painted and ready for final installation. Weathering comprised of fine streaking with the airbrush and a pinpoint oil wash around structural features.

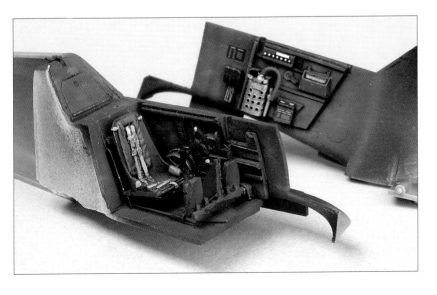

The large resin slab that makes up the cockpit floor and rear bulkhead may be installed almost without modification. In fact, the large casting block adds strength to the weakened fuselage halves.

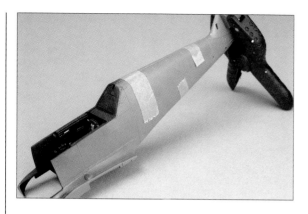

Clamps and tape were used to hold the kit parts together after liquid glue was flowed into the fuselage joins.

Even with large chunks of the fuselage cut away, the fit of the kit was generally excellent. Tamiya tape was stretched along the span of the wing to ensure correct dihedral and also to close any possible gaps at the wing root.

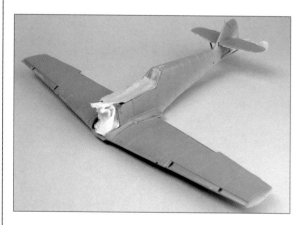

The airframe was painted prior to installation of the engine assembly. The cockpit and rear engine bay were masked with Tamiya tape cut to size and small wads of tissue paper.

Polly Scale Acrylics were used for the main camouflage colours – RLM 79 Desert Sand and RLM 78 Light Blue. The white North African theatre markings were masked and sprayed using Tamiya acrylic XF-2 Flat White.

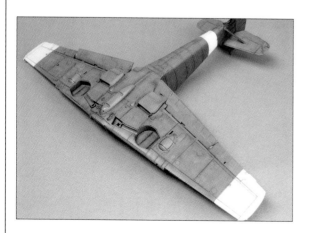

A wash of thinned raw umber oil paint was applied to the upper and lower surfaces of the model to add a little grime and also to subtly highlight panel lines.

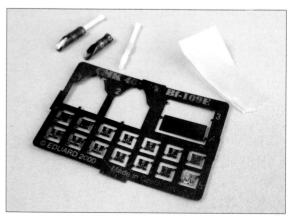

CMK's engine set includes a small photo-etched fret that provides latches and machine-gun shrouds.

starboard side, also removing a thin slice of fuselage below the panel line. A narrow wedge of plastic was glued in place to correct this mistake.

The cockpit was less traumatic. I used KMC's 1/48-scale Bf 109E cockpit, which has now been re-packaged by True Details. This is a well-detailed front office with cast-on cushion and harness for the seat, and impressively three-dimensional sidewalls. Construction and painting presented no challenges, and the big casting block behind the resin cockpit lent strength to the fuselage halves. The new cockpit was trapped between the fuselage halves, and the airframe was quickly assembled.

The wings and rear fuselage were painted and weathered before the engine was installed. Polly Scale paints were used – RLM 79 Desert Sand and RLM 78 Light Blue. When the main colours had dried, the fuselage and wings were masked for the white North African theatre markings.

The model was sprayed with Future in preparation for decals, but the floor polish proved to be temperamental. Instead of a smooth gloss, the surface was covered with satin blotches. A coat of Tamiya Clear covered this unsightly mess and provided a glossy base for decals.

The various subassemblies are brought together for final construction. Note that, at this stage, even the antenna wire has been attached to the mast.

A number of accessories were prepared to display with this model. The bomb trolley is from Revell-Monogram, while the ladder, table and tools were sourced from Eduard figure sets.

Bf 109E fighter-bomber decals are fairly rare, but Hasegawa's Bf 109E-4/7 Trop kit includes one Jabo option. The unique markings were cut from Hasegawa's decal sheet. These were quite thick, but the edges eventually settled down with a couple of applications of Mr Mark Softer, a strong decal solvent. The thick decals also were sliced along panel lines to assist conformity. National markings and a few selected stencils were sourced from various Aeromaster decal sheets.

When the time came to bring the completed engine and airframe sub-assemblies together, something was still not quite right. The engine appeared to be mounted a few millimetres too far forward, and the machine guns seemed to be a millimetre or so too far back. I think that CMK's top engine mounts might be too long. To avoid this problem, I suggest that the resin ammo bins and cowl guns should be installed in the fuselage first, and only then should the engine assembly (including the exhausts and the forward lower cowl) be fitted to the fuselage. That way, the engine mounts can be trimmed to the correct length before they are glued to the airframe.

CMK's propeller assembly presented no such challenges, and looked great when finished. The front of the spinner backplate and the distinctive pitch collars were painted Tamiya XF-16 Flat Aluminium and weathered with a wash of thinned raw umber oil paint to impart the impression of oily metal.

A number of airfield accessories were prepared. I wanted to jack the rear of my Emil up, but I did not have any 1/48-scale trestles. I saw a photo of a Bf 109E-7 in Sicily propped up on fuel drums, so I created a similar arrangement. One of the fuel drums is from Verlinden, while the other is from Tamiya. The small jacks were scratch built from brass rod and strip. The ladder and table are from Eduard figure sets, while the bomb trolley was produced by Revell-Monogram.

The model is depicted jacked up, awaiting maintenance on its engine and machine guns.

ABOVE Unique markings were sourced from Hasegawa's Bf 109E-4/7 kit number JT10. These decals were quite thick but eventually conformed after several applications of progressively stronger decal setting solutions.

BELOW Other decals, including national markings, were scrounged from various Cutting Edge and Eagle Cals sheets.

Further reading and websites

Selected Bf 109V/B/C/D/E references

List compiled by Charles Metz

Beaman, *Messerschmitt Bf 109 in Action (Part 1)* (Aircraft in Action series, No. 44; Squadron/Signal [USA], 1980) – Bf 109B, Bf 109C, Bf 109D, Bf 109E

Beauvais, Kössler, Mayer, and Regel, *Flugerprobungsstellen bis 1945: Johannisthal, Lipsek, Rechlin, Travemünde, Tarnewitz, Peenemünde-West* (Die deutsche Luftfahrt series, No. 27; Bernard & Graefe Verlag [Germany], 1998) – Bf 109 V1, Bf 109 V11

Cerda, *Les Messerschmitt Espagnols: Des Premiers 109 V aux Derniers Buchon* (Hors Série Avions series, No. 5; Editions Lela Presse [France], 1997) – Bf 109 V3, Bf 109B, Bf 109C, Bf 109D, Bf 109E

Ebert, Kaiser, and Peters, *Willy Messerschmitt - Pioneer of Aviation Design* (The History of German Aviation series, No. 3; Schiffer [USA], 1993) – Bf 109 V1, Bf 109 V13, Bf 109 V17, Bf 109B, Bf 109E

Elbied, and Jouineau, *Me 109, Vol. I: From 1936 to 1942* (Planes and Pilots series, No. 1; Historie & Collections [France], 2001) – Bf 109 V1, Bf 109 V3, Bf 109 V7, Bf 109 V13, Bf 109 V14, Bf 109B, Bf 109C, Bf 109D, Bf 109E

Fernández-Sommerau, *Messerschmitt Bf 109 Recognition Manual* (Air War Classics series [unnumbered]; Classic Publications [UK], 2004) – Bf 109 V1, Bf 109B, Bf 109D, Bf 109E

Green, *Augsburg Eagle: The Messerschmitt Bf 109* (Aston Publications [UK], 1987; 144 pages) – Bf 109 V10, Bf 109B, Bf 109C, Bf 109E

Hall, Banyai-Reipl, and Rosch, *Messerschmitt Bf 109* (Warpaint Special series, No. 2; Hall Park Books [UK], 2001) – Bf 109 V1, Bf 109 V3, Bf 109 V4, Bf 109 V7, Bf 109 V9, Bf 109 V15, Bf 109B, Bf 109C, Bf 109D, Bf 109E

Hitchcock, *Messerschmitt 'O-Nine' Gallery* (Monogram Aviation Publications [USA], 1973) – Bf 109 V series, Bf 109B, Bf 109C, Bf 109D, Bf 109E

Hoch, *Die Messerschmitt Me 109 in der Schweizer Flugwaffe: ein Stück Zeitgeschichte* (privately published [Switzerland], 1999) – Bf 109 V1, Bf 109 V7, Bf 109 V9, Bf 109 V13, Bf 109 V14, Bf 109B, Bf 109D, Bf 109E

Kit, and Aders, *Les Messerschmitt sur le Front Méditerranéen* (Editions Atlas [France], 1982) – Bf 109E

Kit, and Payne, *Les Messerschmitt dans la Bataille d'Angleterre: Le Bf 109E* (Editions Atlas [France], 1980) – Bf 109E

Kosin, *The German Fighter since 1915* (Putnam Aeronautical series [unnumbered]; Putnam [UK]) – Bf 109 V1, Bf 109B, Bf 109E

Laureau, *Condor: The Luftwaffe in Spain 1936–1939* (Hikoki [UK], 2000) – Bf 109 V4, Bf 109 V5, Bf 109B, Bf 109C, Bf 109D, Bf 109E

Ledwoch, *Messerschmitt Bf 109 Color* (Wydawnictwo Militaria series [unnumbered]; Militaria [Poland], 1996) – Bf 109B, Bf 109C, Bf 109D, Bf 109E

Maslov, *Messerschmitt Bf 109B-1* (Belaya series, No. 8; M-Hobby [Russia], 1995) – Bf 109B

Merrick, *German Aircraft Interiors 1935–1945: Vol. 1* (German Aircraft Interiors series, No. 1; Monogram Aviation Publications [USA], 1996) – Bf 109 V1, Bf 109B, Bf 109C, Bf 109D, Bf 109E

Messerschmitt Bf 109B-E (Model Art Special Issue series, No. 375; Model Art [Japan], 1991) – Bf 109 V1, Bf 109 V3, Bf 109 V4, Bf 109B, Bf 109C, Bf 109D, Bf 109E

Michulec, *Messerschmitt Bf 109: Part 1* (Monografie series [unnumbered]; AJ Press [Poland], 1998) – Bf 109a (Bf 109 V1), Bf 109 V2, , Bf 109 V3, Bf 109 V4, Bf 109 V7, Bf 109 V8, Bf 109 V10, Bf 109 V15, Bf 109 V17, Bf 109B, Bf 109C, Bf 109D, Bf 109E

Michulec, *Messerschmitt Me 109, pt. 1* (Aircraft Monograph series, No. 16; AJ Press [Poland], 2001) – Bf 109a (Bf 109 V1), Bf 109 V2, Bf 109 V3, Bf 109 V4, Bf 109 V6, Bf 109 V7, Bf 109 V8, Bf 109 V10, Bf 109 V13, Bf 109 V15, Bf 109 V17, Bf 109B, Bf 109C, Bf 109D, Bf 109E

Mombeek, Roba, and Pegg, *Strike in the Balkans, April–May 1941* (Luftwaffe Colours: Jagdwaffe series, Vol. 3, No. 1; Classic Publications [UK], 2003) – Bf 109E

Mombeek, Smith, and Creek, *Birth of the Luftwaffe Fighter Force* (Luftwaffe Colours: Jagdwaffe series, Vol. 1, No. 1; Classic Publications [UK], 1999) – Bf 109 V1, Bf 109B

Mombeek, Smith, and Creek, *The Spanish Civil War* (Luftwaffe Colours: Jagdwaffe series, Vol. 1, No. 2; Classic Publications [UK], 1999) – Bf 109 V3, Bf 109B, Bf 109C, Bf 109D, Bf 109E

Mombeek, Smith, and Creek, *Blitzkrieg and Sitzkrieg* (Luftwaffe Colours: Jagdwaffe series, Vol. 1, No. 3; Classic Publications [UK], 1999) – Bf 109D, Bf 109E

Mombeek, Smith, and Creek, *Attack in the West* (Luftwaffe Colours: Jagdwaffe series, Vol. 1, No. 4; Classic Publications [UK], 2000) – Bf 108B, Bf 109C, Bf 109D, Bf 109E

Mombeek, Wadman, and Creek, *Battle of Britain Phase One, July–August 1940* (Luftwaffe Colours: Jagdwaffe series, Vol. 2, No. 1; Classic Publications [UK], 2001) – Bf 109E

Mombeek, Wadman, and Creek, *Battle of Britain Phase Two, August–September 1940* (Luftwaffe Colours: Jagdwaffe series, Vol. 2, No. 2; Classic Publications [UK], 2001) – Bf 109E

Mombeek, Wadman, and Creek, *Battle of Britain Phase Three, September–October 1940* (Luftwaffe Colours: Jagdwaffe series, Vol. 2, No. 3; Classic Publications [UK], 2001) – Bf 109E

Mombeek, Wadman, and Creek, *Battle of Britain Phase Four, November 1940–June 1941* (Luftwaffe Colours: Jagdwaffe series, Vol. 2, No. 4; Classic Publications [UK], 2002) – Bf 109E

Nohara, and Shiwaku, *Messerschmitt Bf 109E* (Aero Detail series, No. 1; Dai-Nippon Kaiga Co., Ltd. [Japan], 1989) – Bf 109E

Nowarra, *Messerschmitt Bf 109: Aircraft & Legend* (Haynes/Motorbuch Verlag [UK/Germany], 1989) – Bf 109 V1, Bf 109 V3, Bf 109 V4, Bf 109 V5, Bf 109 V6, Bf 109B, Bf 109C, Bf 109D, Bf 109E

Nowarra, *The Messerschmitt 109: A Famous German Fighter* (Harleyford series [unnumbered]; Aero/Harleyford [USA/UK], 1963) – Bf 109 V5, Bf 109 V6, Bf 109 V7, Bf 109 V10, Bf 109 V13, Bf 109B, Bf 109C, Bf 109D, Bf 109E

Nowarra, *Die Deutsche Luftrüstung 1933–1945, Band 3: Flugzeugtypen Henschel – Messerschmitt* (Die Deutsche Luftrüstung series, No. 3; Bernard & Graefe Verlag [Germany], 1993) – Bf 109 V1, Bf 109 V7, Bf 109 V15, Bf 109B, Bf 109C, Bf 109D, Bf 109E

Osché, *The Messerschmitt Bf 109 in Swiss Service/Les Messerschmitt Bf 109 Suisses* (Hors Série Avions series, No. 4; Editions Lela Presse [France], 1996) – Bf 109 V7, Bf 109 V8, Bf 109 V13, Bf 109B, Bf 109D, Bf 109E

Payne, *Messerschmitt Bf 109 into the Battle* (Air Research Publications [UK], 1987) – Bf 109E

Radinger, and Schick, *Messerschmitt Bf 109 A-E* (Schiffer [USA], 1999) – Bf 109 V1, Bf 109 V2, Bf 109 V3, Bf 109 V4, Bf 109 V7, Bf 109 V9, Bf 109 V13, Bf 109 V13 "Weltrekord", Bf 109 V14, Bf 109B, Bf 109C, Bf 109D, Bf 109E

Smith, and Creek, *Me 262: Volume 1* (Classic series, No. 3; Classic Publications [UK], 1998) – Bf 109 V1, Bf 109 V3, Bf 109 V13, Bf 109B

Stapfer, *Messerschmitt Bf 109E* (Walk Around series, No. 34; Squadron/Signal [USA], 2004) – Bf 109E

Websites with Messerschmitt Bf 109 content

The 109 Lair http://www.109lair.com
Falcon's Messerschmitt Hangar http://www.messerschmitt-bf109.de/index-1024.php
Le Messerschmitt 109 http://www.messerschmitt109.com/
HyperScale http://www.hyperscale.com/

Scale model related website including articles and galleries on the Bf 109 in all scales
Modeling Madness http://www.modelingmadness.com
Aircraft Resource Center http://www.aircraftresourcecenter.com
Internet Modeler http://www.internetmodeler.com
Armorama http://www.armorama.com

Index

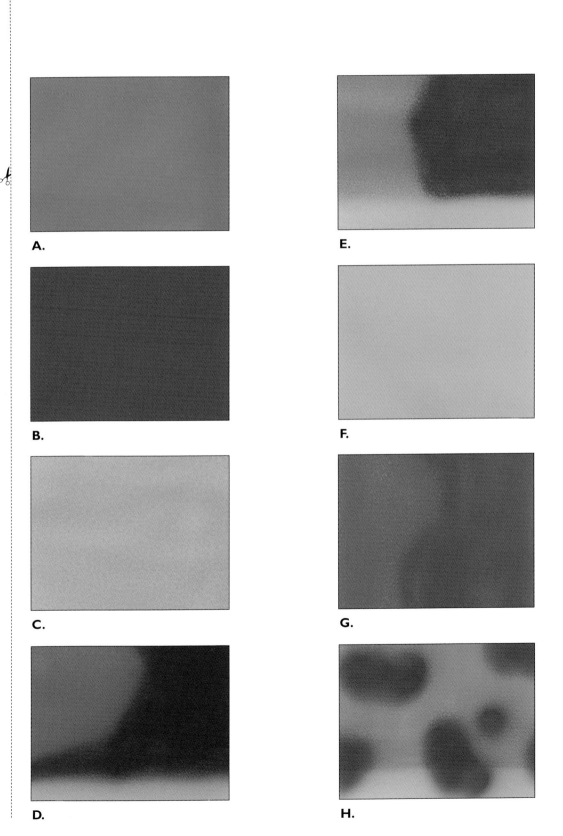

A.

B.

C.

D.

E.

F.

G.

H.

E.

In 1940, the scheme changed to RLM 02 Grey and RLM 71 Dark Green. The lower surface colour of RLM 65 was also brought higher up the fuselage sides.

A.

RLM 02 Grey was used as an overall colour on some early Bf 109s, an interior and cockpit colour, and a disruptive camouflage colour on Bf 109Es from 1940.

F.

RLM 04 Yellow was frequently used on engine cowls, rudders and wing tips as a quick identification colour.

B.

RLM 66 Dark Grey replaced RLM 02 as the standard cockpit colour during the Bf 109E production run, although other interior surfaces retained their RLM 02 finish.

G.

By the end of the Battle of Britain, some Bf 109 units were experimenting with all-grey upper surface camouflage that would eventually evolve into a new mid-war standard.

C.

The earliest Bf 109s sent to Spain wore a translucent coat of zinc chromate that lent a green tinge to the metallic finish.

H.

Luftwaffe desert colours were RLM 78 Light Blue, RLM 79 Tan and RLM 80 Olive Green.

D.

By the outbreak of war, the Messerschmitt Bf 109 wore a finish of RLM 70 Black Green and RLM 71 Dark Green upper surfaces; and RLM 65 Light Blue on lower surfaces.